WRIGLEY FIELD

A Celebration of the Friendly Confines

PHOTOS BY STEPHEN GREEN

TEXT BY MARK JACOB

FOREWORD BY ERNIE BANKS

Contemporary Books

Chicago New York San Francisco Lisbon London Madrid Mexico City
Milan New Delhi San Juan Seoul Singapore Sydney Toronto

The McGraw·Hill Companies

Library of Congress Cataloging-in-Publication Data

Green, Stephen, 1952–   .
       Wrigley Field : a celebration of the friendly confines / photos by Stephen Green, text
by Mark Jacob ; foreword by Ernie Banks.
               p.   cm.
       Includes index.
       ISBN 0-07-138563-0
       1. Wrigley Field (Chicago, Ill.)—History.   2. Chicago Cubs (Baseball team)—History.
I. Jacob, Mark.   II. Title.

GV416.I32 C454   2002
796.357' 06' 877311—dc21   2002067204

5 6 7 8 9 0   KGP/KGP 1 0 9 8 7 6 5 4

ISBN 0-07-138563-0

Jacket photo copyright © Stephen Green

McGraw-Hill books are available at special quantity discounts to use as premiums and sales
promotions, or for use in corporate training programs. For more information, please write to the
Director of Special Sales, Professional Publishing, McGraw-Hill, Two Penn Plaza, New York, NY
10121-2298. Or contact your local bookstore.

This book is printed on acid-free paper.

To my wife, Lisa, whom I met on a magical night at Wrigley, and my daughter, Shae, who loves the park as much as I do

—Stephen Green

To my brothers, Tim, Paul, and Matt, and my sisters, Kathleen and Anne

—Mark Jacob

CONTENTS

FOREWORD

WRIGLEY FIELD ISN'T AN OLD PLACE—it's young at heart, and it gets younger every year. It grows more charming, too, from every angle, and I should know—I've seen the park from lots of different positions: as a Cubs player, a coach, a member of the front office, and, finally, now, as a fan.

The first time I ever went to the park, on September 8, 1953, I didn't have such a great view. I was with the Kansas City Monarchs of the Negro Leagues when I was taken to an office under the stands and given a contract with the Cubs. I signed it, and then I left. That first time at Wrigley was all business. I never even got to see the field.

My second time, I saw the diamond, of course, since I was playing on it. But that wasn't the best place to appreciate Wrigley Field. Not for me, at least. As a player, I shut out all distractions. I played the game like there was nobody there but me. Just me and the ball.

Don't get me wrong—before and after the game, the fans and the atmosphere were great, but during the game, it was just me and the baseball. Even as first-base coach, I was like that. Except I had a better angle on some things. I could look into the dugout, into the eyes of the opposing team, and see how sleepy they were, whether they'd been to Rush Street the night before.

Then, after I hung up my uniform, I joined the Cubs' marketing department as director of group sales. We would go door-to-door in the neighborhood asking people how often they went to the ballpark. We set up tours of the park, so fans could see it inside and out. We even had a group of business students from Northwestern University come to the park to study "the quantitative method of optimal decision making under conditions of uncertainty."

Uncertainty—the Cubs are a perfect case study in that. You never know what's going to happen when you go to the park. Anything could happen any day. In fact, Steven Spielberg should come to Wrigley Field and get a feel for real drama.

My days in the front office made me appreciate the pride that the owners had in the park, the way they're dedicated to taking care of it. To me, and to them, the park is one of the wonders of the world, like the Taj Mahal and the Hanging Gardens of Babylon.

Now, as a fan, I've got the best angle on the ballpark. After all, Wrigley Field is made for the fans. And those Northwestern kids studying the quantitative method aren't the only smart people at Wrigley. I've always thought the Cubs had high-IQ fans, that people who come out to the park are highly intelligent people. It's an education sitting there. The fans talk to each other. They learn things from each other.

Sitting in the stands, you feel like a family. During the seventh-inning stretch, everyone stands up and gets into it. People in Wrigley Field live by the lyrics— "Buy me some peanuts and Cracker Jack, I don't care if I never get back." Baseball is trying to speed up the games, but Cubs fans aren't like that. At Wrigley Field, they're happy to be there, and they stay to the end.

Now the ballpark is nearly 90 years old, almost at the end of its first century, and it's better than ever, young at heart, and ready for the next hundred years.

Let's play two, I say. Let's play two centuries.

—Ernie Banks

ACKNOWLEDGMENTS

THE AUTHORS WISH TO THANK Lena McDonagh, Cubs director of publications, for her patience and wisdom. Jim McArdle, editor of the Cubs' monthly magazine, *Vine Line*, and associate editor Michael Huang offered many helpful suggestions. We thank the entire Cubs family for its cooperation, especially Mark McGuire, Rebecca Polihronis, Samantha Newby, and the grounds crew and security staff. Ed Hartig's command of Cubs history was a vital resource for this book. Rob Taylor and Nick Panos of McGraw-Hill's Contemporary Books lent their talent to the project. Research help was generously provided by Tim Wiles of the National Baseball Hall of Fame in Cooperstown, New York; Steven P. Gietschier of the Sporting News Research Center in St. Louis; and Tim Samuelson, curator of architecture and design at the Chicago Historical Society. Other key players were writer and photo editor Richard Cahan, baseball writer Rob Ehrgott, photographer Sam Bruno, ballhawk Johnny Rosenstein, and beer vendor Rich Harris. The Skokie, Illinois, Public Library; the Chicago Public Library's Harold Washington Library Center; and the *Chicago Tribune* were invaluable resources. Assistance also was provided by groups as diverse as the Harlem Globetrotters and the Norge Ski Club and writers such as Janice Petterchak, biographer of Jack Brickhouse; Joe Ziemba, an expert on the Chicago Cardinals football team; and retired sports columnist Jerome Holtzman, now serving as historian to the commissioner of Major League Baseball. The section on the Chicago Bears would not have been possible without the help of George Halas's grandson Brian McCaskey and Bears fans Donald J. Baron and Matt Baron. Photographic support was provided by Parkway Imaging, Canon USA, Kodak Professional Services, and Fuji Film USA. We are grateful to photo and memorabilia collectors David Phillips, Dan Knoll of Best of Yesterday, and Eddie and Audre Gold of AU Sports Memorabilia. The Brace family—former Cubs official photographer George Brace, his wife, Agnes, their daughter Mary, and their granddaughter Debbie Miller—opened their photo treasures to us. The authors also wish to thank their wives and children for their support.

Much of the text of this book is based on original interviews and research, but we have also taken advantage of the wealth of baseball literature and lore. Three books have been particularly informative: *Banks to Sandberg to Grace* by Carrie Muskat, *The Million-to-One Team* by George Castle, and *A Day at the Park* by William Hartel. The notes at the end of this book attempt to credit the sources of the many quotations and anecdotes that are not original to this book.

ABOUT THE PHOTOS

Stephen Green began photographing Wrigley Field under an Illinois Arts Council grant in 1981. The next year, he became the Cubs' official photographer, a position he has held ever since. The vast majority of the photos in this book are his. But America's greatest ballpark has been photographed more often than Marilyn Monroe, and a number of photographs from the George Brace Collection and other archives are included in this book to tell the whole story. It's easy to tell which were taken by Green and which were taken by others: all of the color photos are Green's. Photos taken by others are black-and-white. A complete list of credits for the photos not taken by Green is included in the back of this book.

INTRODUCTION

THIS BALLPARK WE LOVE IS MANY THINGS. It is a museum and a hot dog joint. It is a day at the beach and a night in the rain. It is a national monument and a neighborhood hangout. It is a circus and a cathedral.

It is a delightful contradiction. On the one hand, it is a time capsule, infused with history. On the other hand, it maintains an everyday familiarity and a willingness to change at a moment's notice. Wrigley Field is both a celebrity and a good friend. It is priceless jewelry that you can wear.

The ballpark, nearly nine decades old, has refused to age gracefully. It has refused to age, period. It isn't a bronze statue serving as a pigeon perch in the city square. It's a working ballpark that has stayed vital by changing and changing and changing again, reshaping itself to meet the demands of each new age.

For a park so steeped in tradition, and in elegance, it has been willing to try all sorts of new ideas. In fact, its crazy schemes have been so successful that they are no longer considered crazy schemes—they have become baseball's cherished traditions.

Wrigley Field was the first park to let fans keep foul balls. The first to have an organist. The first to build a permanent concession stand. And when the Bears played at Wrigley, as they did for half a century, the ballpark was the proving

ground for George Halas's bold innovations with the T formation and the man in motion. Wrigley Field has always been revolutionary.

But it's always been a curmudgeon, too. Along with the firsts, Wrigley has a notable "last": for 40 years, it was the lone holdout for day-only baseball. The ballpark has plenty of "not yets," too: no JumboTron scoreboard—yet. No hidden bullpen built into the outfield stands—yet. No costumed animal mascots—yet.

Wrigley Field has always known how to change and how to stay the same. The ballpark has remade itself over and over, responding to what the fans needed and wanted. But Wrigley Field is special for more than its ability to adapt and survive.

Wrigley is beloved because it is a refuge, a place where the workweek disappears, where homework doesn't exist. It is a haven, an escape.

If the ballpark were surrounded by acres of farmland or parkland, by rolling fields of green grass, it wouldn't be as special. Instead, it's shoehorned into a city, besieged by concrete, suffocated by smog. It's an oasis.

If the ballpark were in a temperate climate, where year-round sunshine were guaranteed, it wouldn't be as special. Instead, it's in a city showered by sleet, battered by winds. But on certain summer days—not many, not enough to spoil the Midwestern stoics who worship here—the park is a festival of green, bathed in sunlight, massaged by the lake's soothing breeze.

Wrigley Field is our reward for surviving Chicago's winter. Its bright, shining days are rare, which makes them all the more precious and magical.

The place is a shrine, and it's a museum, but it's like no other. At what other shrine, at what other museum, can you boo, scream, heckle, groan, high-five a complete stranger, eat popcorn, and drink beer?

At no other. Only at Wrigley Field.

"To me there's always been something magical about Wrigley Field. I refer to the ballpark as the dowager queen of the National League. I refer to the lights as a lady in black in evening, wearing pearls. Every time I come to this ballpark, I seem to feel and see another image, and, above all, the enthusiasm of the crowd. It's just a very special place."

—BROADCASTER VIN SCULLY

Here's what sets Wrigley Field apart: the history, the vines,

the bleachers, the scoreboard, and the endless debate

over day or night games.

1 THE FRIENDLY CONFINES

THE HISTORY

The irregular city block bounded by Clark, Addison, Waveland, and Sheffield was always meant to be some sort of park. In the 19th century, the site was a picnic grounds—a woodsy, hilly place with rabbits, squirrels, pine trees, and a huge bell to summon worshippers to nearby St. Mark's Lutheran Church.

Nature was quickly routed by the burgeoning city. From 1891 to 1910, the area was the home of the Theological Seminary of the Evangelical Lutheran Church. In 1914, the church buildings came down and a different kind of shrine went up— the ballpark for the Chicago Federals (or "Chi Feds"), the local entry in the upstart Federal League, which sought to compete with the American and National Leagues.

The team was owned by Charles "Lucky Charlie" Weeghman, an Indiana native who came to Chicago as a waiter in the 1890s and built his own chain of quick-lunch restaurants. At Weeghman's eateries, customers sat at "one-armed" chairs, somewhat like grammar school desks, so that more diners could be squeezed in. At one Weeghman restaurant downtown, 35,000 customers were served daily.

Zachary Taylor Davis, chief architect
of Wrigley Field

Weeghman liked to work fast, and his ballpark reflected that. The park went up in less than seven weeks, despite a two-day labor strike, and was ready for business four days before Opening Day.

It was designed by the firm of Davis & Davis, run by two brothers, Zachary Taylor Davis and Charles G. Davis, from Aurora, Illinois, west of Chicago. The visionary was Zachary, who also was the architect of Comiskey Park, on the South Side. The construction took 490 workers, cost $250,000, and required four thousand yards of soil and four acres of bluegrass.

Weeghman's "edifice of beauty," as he called it at the groundbreaking, joined a new generation of ballparks. Gone were the rickety wooden firetraps of the previous century; here was the modern stadium of concrete and steel. Wrigley Field, built in 1914, was part of a renaissance that included Philadelphia's Shibe Park (1908), Pittsburgh's Forbes Field (1908), Chicago's Comiskey Park (1910), Boston's Fenway Park (1912), Cincinnati's Crosley Field (1912), Detroit's Tiger Stadium (1912), Brooklyn's Ebbets Field (1913), and Boston's Braves Field (1913). Today, only Fenway and Wrigley survive as major league ballparks.

The groundbreaking for what would become Wrigley Field. In attendance are (from left) Chicago Federals owner Charles Weeghman, Federal League president Jim Gilmore, and Joe Tinker, player-manager for the "Chi Feds."

The first game ever at Weeghman's showcase was a victory for the home team, 9–1 vs. the Kansas City Packers. The park was built to hold only 14,000 fans, but 20,000 crowded inside to witness the birth of the ballpark.

Although Zachary Davis created the baseball treasure we enjoy today, it would be wrong to give him all the credit. The ballpark was built as a single-deck stadium, and it has undergone a long succession of improvements over the years. In fact, the first tweaking took place almost immediately: nine home runs were hit in the first three-game series, and the outfield wall was moved back 25 feet in left and almost 50 feet in left-center.

Wrigley Field is born on April 23, 1914, as the home of the Federal League's Chicago team.

At first, it wasn't called Wrigley Field, of course. It was known by a variety of names, including the North Side Ball Park, the Federal League Ball Park, and Weeghman Park. In 1915, it was called Whales Park, after the team changed its name from the Chi Feds to the Whales. The name Whales was chosen in a fan contest, but the rationale has escaped into the vapor of history. D. J. Eichoff, whose nickname was chosen out of 350 entries, noted cryptically at the time that "the best commercial whales are found on the North Side." Perhaps the name Whales was supposed to connote bigness, or perhaps it was a reference to the verb form of whale, which means "to lash, thrash, or drub." Or perhaps the name Whales was a play on the ballpark's location on Waveland, an avenue so named because it used to flood when Lake Michigan got rambunctious.

The Whales were ambitious rivals to the American League's White Sox and the National League's Cubs, and Whales Park's capacity was increased by four thousand in 1915. Some of Weeghman's promotional methods raised eyebrows, such as his "*Eastland* Sufferers' Day," held five days after the pleasure ship *Eastland* overturned in the Chicago River, killing 812 people. Weeghman donated admission fees to the families of survivors and hired chorus girls to sell flowers at the gate. The rival Cubs denounced him as a publicity hound and an exploiter of the dead.

Other teams in the Federal League lacked the aggressive marketing and deep pockets of Weeghman, and the league collapsed after the 1915 season, in which the Whales won the league title. The league's demise was no tragedy to Lucky Charlie. As part of the death benefits, he and nine other investors were allowed to buy the Cubs from Charles Taft, the half brother of former president William Howard Taft. Whales Park became Weeghman Park again.

Among Weeghman's partners in buying the Cubs was a chewing gum entrepreneur named William Wrigley Jr., who used to brag that he could sell "pianos to armless men in Borneo." Expelled from school in Philadelphia at age 12, Wrigley had left home, selling newspapers in New York City and soap in rural Pennsylvania. In 1891, he headed west to Chicago, and soon after, at age 30, he got into the chewing gum business, then known as the "chicle" business. In 1915, he collected addresses out of phone books around the country and mailed four free

5

"The real Cub fans are on the West Side. Moving the team's base to the North Side is a bad idea."

—Charles Murphy, the Cubs' deposed president, criticizing the 1916 move to Clark and Addison from the West Side Grounds

6

sticks of chewing gum to 1.5 million people. He did the same thing again in 1919 with a bigger address list—7 million.

Weeghman and Wrigley's new team moved from the West Side Grounds at Polk and Lincoln (now Wolcott), which had been its home since 1893. The change of venue was adorned with the pomp of the time: a mile-long parade from Grant Park to the North Side ballpark. The Cubs' first game there, on April 20, 1916, was a sign of good things to come, a 7–6 victory over Cincinnati in eleven innings. The park was quite a zoo that first year, with a real bear cub named Joa (named after the initials of Cubs part owner J. Ogden Armour) living in a cage at Clark and Addison for part of the season. In 1916, Weeghman ordered his ushers to let fans keep foul balls, a policy that soon spread to the rest of the major leagues.

The next several decades were an illustrious era for the team and the ballpark. William Veeck Sr., a sportswriter who wrote under the pseudonym Bill Bailey at the *Chicago American*, wrote a series of articles on how to improve the Cubs, and Wrigley was so impressed that he hired Veeck in 1918 to help run the organization. Veeck was a visionary, startlingly honest with the press and full of progressive spirit. He was instrumental in gaining acceptance for *Tribune* sports editor Arch Ward's idea of an all-star game. Veeck defied baseball's conventional wisdom by hiring a career minor leaguer, Joe McCarthy, as manager, a move that carried the Cubs to the World Series in 1929. Not all of Veeck's innovations were instantly embraced: it took until the 1990s for Major League Baseball to catch up with his idea of interleague play.

As Veeck came in, Weeghman was going out. Struggling in his restaurant business, Lucky Charlie began selling his Cubs stock to Wrigley and eventually was out of the picture, taking a $3 million bath on baseball. In 1920, Weeghman Park became Cubs Park, and the next year Wrigley became majority owner of the team. Two months after gaining control of the Cubs, Wrigley bought an entire island— Catalina Island, off the coast of southern California—without ever seeing the place. It would be the Cubs' spring training home for decades.

It was quickly becoming clear that Wrigley's Chicago ballpark would have to be expanded. In 1918, the Cubs reached the World Series and made a decision that

At the height of success after clinching the pennant in 1929 are (from left) Cubs owner William Wrigley Jr., manager Joseph McCarthy, and team president William Veeck Sr.

would be unthinkable today—they played their home World Series games at Comiskey Park because the South Side park had more seats.

Zachary Taylor Davis was called back after the 1922 season to renovate his creation. The work cost $300,000, more than it had taken to build the park eight years earlier. The entire field was moved 60 feet to the southwest. The pitcher's mound today is where home plate used to be. Workers put rollers under the seats behind home plate and moved them back, toward the corner of Clark and Addison, so that there was room to build more box seats. They also put rollers under the left-field stands and moved them toward Waveland Avenue. In 1923, the Cubs also added seats in the grandstands and built bleachers across the length of the outfield. Capac-

ity reached 20,000. The playing dimensions were 325 feet to left field, 447 to center, and 318 to right.

The bleachers in left proved too close for the pitchers' comfort. In 1925, the New York Giants hit five home runs in one game, and the Cubs responded by tearing out most of the left-field bleachers in midseason, leaving only a small section in left-center, known as the "jury box."

In 1926, the Wrigley family attached its name to the park. That wasn't all that the Wrigleys attached: they began building an upper deck and making other major renovations, with the help of the architecture firm of Graham, Anderson, Probst & White, which designed the Wrigley Building and Merchandise Mart downtown. In 1927, Wrigley Field must have looked lopsided: the left-field side of the

A throng of 43,332 attends a May 31, 1936, doubleheader against Pittsburgh. The catwalk shown here, built in 1929, was used for VIPs and press photographers. The catwalk in the left-field grandstand was used as a football press box for Bears games.

upper deck was open, but the right-field side wasn't ready until the next season. Still, in '27, the Cubs became the first National League team to pass one million in attendance in a season. In 1929, when the Cubs next won the National League pennant, the gate was a major league record 1,485,166. The largest crowd in Wrigley Field history was June 27, 1930—a throng of 51,556. The paid attendance was only 19,748; most of those in attendance were there for Ladies Day and other ticket giveaways.

The '30s was the Cubs' last decade of dominance on the field, and it was when the two men who had brought the park into national prominence, William Wrigley and William Veeck, died. It was also the decade in which their sons, Philip Knight Wrigley and Bill Veeck, transformed the ballpark into the gem we enjoy today.

The only bequest in William Wrigley's will was giving the Cubs to his son. In later years, when there was public pressure on the Wrigleys to sell the team, there would be rumors that P. K. had made a deathbed promise in 1932 to keep the team for his entire life. Whether or not that vow was made, P. K. Wrigley did indeed keep the team for the rest of his life.

P. K. Wrigley was a remarkably high-minded and eccentric owner. Determined to preserve the family image of the park, he instructed radio announcers to call it "beautiful Wrigley Field." He spent millions on upkeep of the park when critics were urging him to spend the money on ballplayers instead. He is the primary reason why the Cubs haven't won a World Series since 1908—and also the primary reason why Wrigley Field has survived to this day.

The younger Wrigley cared deeply for the fans, though he was so shy that he often avoided being around them. He once told an interviewer, "My ambition is to go live in a cave somewhere with no telephones and a big rock over the door." He didn't attend the 1962 All-Star Game at Wrigley Field.

He took bizarre actions, such as paying $5,000 to a man who claimed he could put a hex on the Cubs' opponents. But he also showed an impressive lack of greed, bringing bigger, more comfortable chairs into the box-seat area even though it reduced the park's capacity because only eight seats would fit in a box instead of ten. (The "box" for which "box seats" got their name was a railed–off section with folding chairs inside. At Wrigley, the railings and folding chairs disappeared in the '60s when the Cubs put in permanent seats.) The box seats became a point of embarrassing contrast between Wrigley and George Halas, whose Chicago Bears used the park during football season. The Bears earned public scorn by refusing to use Wrigley's 21-inch-wide chairs. Halas, who had far fewer home dates in which

Until 1937, "standing room only" often meant standing in designated areas along the outfield wall. A hit that bounced into the crowd would be declared a ground-rule double. Note the "jury box," the leftover section of the left-field grandstand after the rest of it was torn down in 1925.

On Opening Day 1937, players take their warm-ups. It was the last season for the old scoreboard, with its Wrigley "stick men." The Baby Ruth candy sign behind the bleachers was a constant reminder of Babe Ruth's "Called Shot" home run at Wrigley five years earlier. The Prager beer sign set a precedent: there is a billboard at that location today.

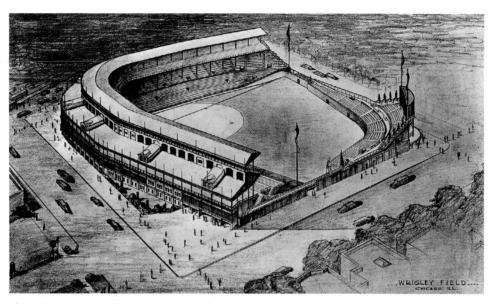

The 1937–38 renovation was overseen by the Holabird & Root architecture firm, which had previously designed Soldier Field and the Chicago Board of Trade Building.

to make his money, insisted on using 15-inch-wide, less comfortable chairs to boost capacity for football.

Wrigley's conscientious housekeeping did not go unnoticed. As Ed Burns of the *Chicago Tribune* put it in 1937: "There's always some painting being done at Wrigley Field. The paint is so extensive, in fact, that groundskeepers after each game have to eject Ira Hartnett, a paint salesman, who lives in constant terror that someone will chisel the account."

The Cubs reached the World Series three times in the 1930s, and most of the charming fixtures of Wrigley Field made their first big-league appearance then.

Early in that amazing decade, the Cubs put up the marquee at Clark and Addison, which now reads "Wrigley Field: Home of Chicago Cubs." At first, it wasn't painted the trademark red that we see today. In fact, it wasn't painted at all. "It was

For the 1935 World Series, the Chicago Transit Authority's streetcars whisked fans down

"With Wrigley Field, you get a very elegant and high-quality simplicity, which never got dated. Those '60s ballparks look like something out of the '60s. The simplicity of Wrigley gave it a timeless modernism."

—Tim Samuelson, curator of architecture and design, Chicago Historical Society

16

a fern-green porcelain," recalled retired Cubs executive E. R. "Salty" Saltwell, "the reason for that being that it would stand the weather better than a painted surface." But by 1960, said Saltwell, "the porcelain finish was getting real dull," and that's when it was painted. The Cubs considered making it blue but finally settled on the bright red.

Only a year after P. K. Wrigley took over, William Veeck died, but Wrigley was supported by Veeck's young, energetic son, Bill, in fashioning the renovations of 1937–38 that created the current bleachers, scoreboard, and ivy-covered outfield walls. One facet of the renovation that hasn't survived was a row of Chinese elm

Wrigley Field's scoreboard, new at the time, is set up with a clock for the football season.

Fans line up at the ballpark in the mid-'40s, the last time the marquee could feature the phrase "National League champions." The coal bins in the background were removed around 1960.

18

P. K. Wrigley (right) and Bill Veeck unveil plans for expanding a different Wrigley Field—the one in Los Angeles—in 1955. Veeck was working as a consultant for the Cubs at the time, checking out the West Coast for possible major league expansion that would include use of Los Angeles's Wrigley Field. It didn't work out to the Wrigleys' benefit, however: Wrigley West, the home of the Pacific Coast League's Los Angeles Angels, hosted a major league team for only one year, 1961, when the Angels joined the American League. The ballpark was demolished in 1966.

trees in the back of the bleachers, four on each side of the scoreboard. The elm leaves were no match for the winds off the lake, and after replacing the trees several times with the same result, the Cubs scrapped the idea.

Other than the Chinese elms, the Wrigley Field we see today is very similar to the park that was unveiled in the late '30s. The outfield dimensions are the same: 353 feet to right, 400 to center, and 355 to left.

The Wrigleys had built a treasure that would endure. Unfortunately, they began fielding lousy teams that wouldn't last—but would only *finish* last.

World War II redrew the map of the world and changed the landscape of Wrigley Field as well. The war dissuaded the Cubs from installing lights (more on that later), and it dried up the supply of imported German peat moss that grounds superintendent Bobby Dorr had been using on the field. It also inspired such promotions as "Aluminum Day." Because of a severe shortage of aluminum, the Cubs offered a free ticket to any woman who brought a piece of the metal to the ballpark.

On September 24, 1943, the Cubs established their all-time low in single-game attendance: 314 fans. Two seasons later, they changed their starting time from 3 P.M. to 1:30 on weekdays and 2 P.M. on weekends to accommodate nighttime war workers.

The Cubs' most recent World Series appearance came in 1945, when the war had depleted major league rosters. The Cubs' opponent was the Detroit Tigers, and *Chicago Sun* columnist Warren Brown declared: "I don't think either team can win it." The Tigers managed to prove him wrong, though, with possible help from something that became known as the Billy Goat curse. A Chicago tavern owner, William Sianis, had brought his pet goat to Wrigley Field for the Series and had attempted to gain admittance, because he had a ticket for the goat. Ushers turned away the goat, worried about its smell and lack of social graces. Sianis promptly put a curse on the Cubs, and after they lost, he sent a telegram to Wrigley that read: "Who stinks now?"

Over the years, there have been attempts to lift the curse. In 1981, Sianis's son, Sam, brought a goat to a game and was admitted. In 1984 and 1986, the goat came back. In 1994, when the Cubs failed to win a home game in April, Sianis and his goat were invited yet again. But hexes are like ink on white rugs: they take hold with ease but are removed with great difficulty. In any case, Sianis's pet became a convenient scapegoat for the folly to come.

The next two decades were grim ones for the Cubs and their ballpark, with attendance goosed only by special events, such as Jackie Robinson's Chicago debut in 1947, a record for Wrigley Field paid attendance for baseball: 46,572.

After the 1948 season, Wrigley took out a newspaper ad to apologize for his team's last-place finish. But they finished last in 1949, too.

20

Sam Sianis, owner of Chicago's Billy Goat Tavern, brings his goat to the park in 1994 in an effort to lift the Billy Goat curse.

The club, which had been so pioneering in stadium renovations in the past, tried new tricks that failed to work. One was a "Speed-Walk," a moving walkway to carry fans from the concourse to the upper deck. Billed as a mechanical marvel, it became a repairman's nightmare in the late '50s. "We had difficulty maintaining it, so finally we shut it down around 1960," Saltwell recalled. Also tried, and scrapped, in the '50s was the use of loudspeakers to broadcast Jack Brickhouse's television play-by-play directly into a section of the left-field grandstand.

Wrigley's tinkering didn't occur solely in the grandstands. Having failed to find a winning manager—having even made manager Charlie Grimm and radio broadcaster Lou Boudreau trade jobs—Wrigley decided in late 1960 to do without a manager altogether and have the team run by a "College of Coaches," an eight-man coaching staff that would rotate through the major and minor leagues. The innovation was widely ridiculed and doomed to failure.

Wrigley also decided to borrow an idea from colleges and hire an athletic director in the early '60s. His choice was retired Air Force Colonel Robert Whitlow, whose short tenure is most remembered for the "Whitlow Fence," an 8-foot-high, 64-foot-wide wire screen behind the center-field wall that was designed to improve the hitters' background but cheated sluggers of home runs and was soon removed.

In 1962, Cubs attendance dropped to 609,802, the lowest in the majors. For a five-year period in the early '60s, the Cubs kept the upper deck closed for all weekday games.

The good news was that it was easy to get a seat on the day of a game (the Cubs always held 22,000 upper-deck and bleacher seats for day-of-game sales only), and it was also true that it was a great place for a mother to come for Ladies Day, with her ticket free and the kids' tickets discounted. She could even bring in a picnic lunch for the kids and get no guff from the vendors. The bad news was that the ballpark and the Cubs were becoming irrelevant to baseball. They had become a comedy club. In those years, only "Mr. Cub" kept the team viable. "Without Ernie Banks," said rival manager Jimmy Dykes, "the Cubs would finish in Albuquerque."

"Children have sat at the knees of their grandfather and listened to him tell of the time the Cubs were in the World Series. And they have marked it off to just another fantasy by the old gaffer, like the depth of the snowfall in the year of the great blizzard."

—Jack Griffin,
Chicago Sun-Times

21

Two ideas that never quite worked at Wrigley Field: the Chinese elm trees in the bleachers and the Speed-Walk escalator in the grandstand

In fact, the phrase "Friendly Confines" was born out of the Cubs' frustration. As Banks tells it, the team was flying home in the late '50s after a brutal road trip. The mood was grim, but Banks and a teammate and friend, Jerry Kindall, were happy to be going home. "I said, 'Jerry, we're going home, where people are friendly, back to the friendly confines.' And Jerry just smiled and said, 'Ah, the friendly confines of Wrigley Field.'"

Cubs Hall of Famer Billy Williams remembers the down days at Wrigley. "When I first came here, of course, we weren't drawing too many people here," he said. "We used to have like six, seven thousand people a game. Things began to change in 1966 when Leo first came here."

Leo "the Lip" Durocher snapped the Cubs out of their mediocrity and created one of the most beloved teams in their history. The 1969 Cubs, featuring Williams, Banks, and Ron Santo, appeared destined to win the pennant, only to collapse in September and fall to the New York Mets, who won 38 of their last 49 games.

The team had failed again, but the ballpark was back on the map. The upper deck was rebuilt in 1968–71. In 1970, the Cubs spent $750,000 on ballpark repairs.

Fans thought 1969 was just the start of good things, but the team stumbled through the '70s. In those years, P. K. Wrigley used to attend the games incognito. He would have his chauffeur drop him off a few blocks from the park, and he'd walk in, dressed casually, and sit in the left-field bleachers. It's a good bet that he heard himself cursed quite a bit.

P.K. and his wife, Helen, died within two months of each other in 1977. Their son Bill faced $40 million in inheritance taxes, and speculation of a sale of the team and the ballpark was rampant. McDonald's owner Ray Kroc had offered to buy the team in 1973. Halas had made the same offer decades earlier. Various entrepreneurs were maneuvering to make a bid when the time came.

A Wrigley Field fan banner mimicked the Wrigley Doublemint gum jingle: "Double your pleasure, double your fun, sell the Cubs in eighty-one!"

And that's exactly what the Wrigley family did, without taking bids. The Wrigleys approached Tribune Company, owner of the *Chicago Tribune* newspaper and WGN radio and television stations, because of its strong local ties, and the deal was done.

On June 16, 1981, after 60 years of exclusive Wrigley ownership, Bill Wrigley announced the team's sale for $20.5 million.

Tribune Company quickly made improvements to the ballpark, such as adding electronic message boards to the scoreboard and marquee, building a gift shop near the main entrance, and constructing the Stadium Club and the Friendly Confines Café.

The new owner's timing was perfect. Among those who witnessed the early-'80s boom market was Cubs ticket manager Frank Maloney, who confessed that "the whole takeoff in Cubs tickets has just amazed me."

According to Maloney, there were a number of factors. "We had the airwaves," he said. "Cable TV was just really starting, and if you had cable TV, you had the Cubs and the Braves. . . . And that made legions of Cubs fans everywhere.

"We had Harry Caray. He was tremendously important to this franchise as a salesman." Maloney also noted, "We're in an age of nostalgia, and as this park gets older, it becomes more valuable because of nostalgia.

"Another factor: the neighborhood dramatically changed. When I came here in 1981, this neighborhood was—you couldn't tell which way it was going to go. You couldn't even tell if it was going to become a slum . . . and then all the yuppies moved in here and this became Boomtown USA, the street, bars, restaurants. . . . There's a whole eight-hour day here, if you want it."

Maloney and others believe that a major factor in the continued popularity of Wrigley Field was the 1984 team, which came within three innings of reaching the World Series.

The highlight of that season was the "Sandberg game," June 23, 1984, vs. the St. Louis Cardinals at Wrigley Field, televised on NBC's *Game of the Week*. Cubs second baseman Ryne Sandberg homered twice off the major leagues' best reliever, former Cub Bruce Sutter, and the second homer sent the game into extra innings, in which the Cubs prevailed 12–11. It was an electric Saturday afternoon, Wrigley at its best.

Pitcher Rick Sutcliffe, who was familiar with Wrigley Field from his days with the Dodgers, joined the Cubs in the middle of the mania.

It was only midseason, but Ryne Sandberg's exploits called for a home-plate celebration during the "Sandberg game" in 1984. Greeting him after his second home run of the game are pitching coach Billy Connors (3), manager Jim Frey, and teammate Dave Owen.

"When I came back here in '84, my memories were '79, '80, and '81, which were bad ball clubs and not a big crowd. It was always a neat place to be. But there wasn't that much excitement as far as the team was concerned. My first game here was a Friday against the Cardinals, and then Saturday it was Sandberg's day, the Sutter homers, and I remember after the game, coming outside, and that was [my wife] Robin's first game, and she was crying and so excited, and she said, 'Are all

the games like this here?' and I went, 'No,' and then I had to pitch the next day, and that was when I shut out the Cardinals, with 14 strikeouts, and it was just like, it was one of those weekends that you just never, ever forget, and I know that the fans here don't forget it, because you felt something happening."

And it's been happening ever since, with huge demand for seats in Wrigley Field. Between 1984 and '85, season-ticket sales jumped from 7,500 to 25,000.

That jump in demand was quite a windfall for Tribune Company, but it also put pressure on the big corporation. Can a publicly held corporation, which must answer to its stockholders, dare to follow its baseball hunches? Certainly it can't hire a Svengali to put a $5,000 hex on the opposition, but can it take a chance on an iffy pitcher or a supposedly washed-up hitter?

One thing it could do—and did—was renovate the ballpark.

In 1984, the Cubs built a new home clubhouse so that players no longer had to shower in shifts. Two years later, the Cubs replaced the catwalks leading from the grandstands to the bleachers, putting in seats—a family section in left and a group section in right.

In 1988, Tribune Company finally won the battle to install lights in the park, but not before a bruising fight. Virtually every recent attempt to renovate or "modernize" the park has been met with fierce resistance.

The Cubs joined the era of skyboxes in 1988–89 by building 67 "mezzanine suites" under the upper deck. And plans are in the works to expand the bleachers, redo the bleacher entrance, and even build a Cubs Hall of Fame.

The main achievement of Wrigley Field in recent years has been to show stadium designers that unique ballparks survive, while cookie-cutter stadiums get replaced. The Wrigley influence is evident in a host of modern sports venues, where architects have built in quirkiness and special features in the form of pirate ships and swimming pools.

As Cubs broadcaster Chip Caray put it, "Whether you go to Pittsburgh or Houston, or St. Louis with their plans for the new ballpark, or Camden Yards in Baltimore, or Turner Field in Atlanta, all of them—every single one of them—took a design cue or more from Wrigley Field. This place is almost 100 years old.

It's in better shape now than it was 20 years ago when the Tribune Company bought the ballpark. So the fact that we're living in a society where everyone's looking to the future, the fact that modern baseball is looking 100 years into its past to come up with the magic formula, to me says it all.

"This is it. This is the answer. This is the magic formula," Caray said. "This is your prom date. This is your high school prom date. You never forget."

THE VINES

The ivy is Wrigley Field's most recognizable signature, and the finest expression of the Wrigleys' philosophy that the ballfield should be a lush "park," not a sterile "stadium."

The idea for the ivy was a collaboration between P. K. Wrigley and Bill Veeck as part of the transformation of the ballpark in 1937–38.

"In planning the construction of the new bleachers," Veeck recalled, "he [Wrigley] decided that an outdoor, woodsy motif was definitely called for. Since I had always admired the ivy-covered bleacher walls at Perry Stadium in Indianapolis, I suggested that we appropriate the idea for ourselves."

Another influence, according to some reports, was a wisteria-covered wall at a Pasadena, California, stadium where the White Sox held their spring training in the '30s.

Veeck planned to plant ivy at the end of the 1937 season so that it would come in strong the next spring. But Wrigley called him before the last home series of the season to say that he had invited people to the park to see the new ivy. So Veeck had to scramble.

"One evening, we went north to a place called Clavey's Corners, and we purchased ivy and bittersweet," said Veeck. The total in Veeck's shopping cart: 350 Japanese bittersweet plants and 200 Boston ivy plants.

"We ran some copper wire up the wall and laced the bittersweet with the ivy. Ultimately, the ivy took over."

27

The ivy wasn't always there. It just seems that way. Here, workers string up the vines near the end of the 1937 season.

People in the stands love the ivy. But not everyone on the field feels the same way about it.

Lou Novikoff, the "Mad Russian" who played left field for the Cubs in the '40s, had a phobia about the vines, a fear that manager Charlie Grimm took great pains to dispel.

"I thought at first that he was susceptible to hay fever," Grimm said, "so I got me some samples of goldenrod and proved to Lou that the vines weren't that. He seemed relieved, but next time a guy hit a ball over his head he stayed farther away from the vines than ever."

Grimm consulted other Cubs execs, and they came up with the theory that Novikoff thought the vines were poison ivy.

"So I took him out again, and this time, when I was sure Mr. Wrigley wasn't looking, I pulled a bunch of the vines off the wall and rubbed them all over my

face and hands. I even chewed a couple of the leaves to prove they couldn't harm anyone. All Novikoff had to say was that he wondered what kind of a smoke they would make. But he wouldn't go near 'em to find out."

Novikoff wasn't the only major leaguer bedeviled by the vines. Even the Pirates' Roberto Clemente, one of the most graceful outfielders of all time, had his struggles. Once, he reached into the ivy and came up throwing—except he had an empty cup in his hand instead of the ball.

Over the years, outfielders have developed countermeasures. In the '70s, the Cubs' Jose Cardenal hid extra balls in the ivy. In 1948, Boston Braves leftfielder Jeff Heath pretended to lose Phil Cavarretta's hit in the ivy, when the ball was resting at Heath's feet all along. Cavarretta thought he had an inside-the-park home run, but umpire Jocko Conlon declared it a ground-rule double. The fans declared it a travesty, showering the field with beer bottles (yes, they sold ballpark beer in glass bottles back then).

Cubs Hall of Famer Billy Williams had his struggles with the vines. "Sometimes they gave you a cushion, but sometimes you could hit one of those big vines and it doesn't feel that good. You know, when you look from [a distance], you think that there's a cushion out there, but you know, they've been there for a long time and you have some big, ropy-like vines out there, which are plastered to the fence, and when you hit that, you've got a headache."

Former Cubs rightfielder Andre Dawson developed a strategy: "You have to play the ivy on the walls. For instance, the ivy in center is much thicker than the ivy down the lines, so the ball bounces back softer in center. You have to allow for that."

A ball that's stuck in the ivy is a ground-rule double. If it bounces out, it's a live ball. Outfielders are supposed to signal when the ball is lost in action (see photo on next page).

"If they ever cut the ivy down, they'll find a hundred baseballs in there."

—Andre Dawson

32

The ball also comes off the wall harder early in the season, when the ivy isn't in bloom. Veteran Cubs outfielders have to become students of the vines.

Even more studious is Cubs head groundskeeper Roger Baird.

"A lot of people don't realize how much abuse those vines get. It's not so much during the game; it's during batting practice. You think of how many baseballs hit those vines, how many get broken. . . . You've got your bleacher fans spilling beer on 'em and everything else. They take a lot of abuse. We really try to keep an eye on 'em and keep people away from 'em.

"Everybody wants a leaf," Baird said. "You gave everyone a leaf, you'd have no more vines left."

There are also the natural enemies.

"Vines do not like cool, damp weather," Baird said. "You get major leaf spot, which is a very dangerous thing. It can burn all your leaves out."

And then there's the wear and tear that the ivy has on the brick wall behind it.

In the mid-'80s, the Cubs made major repairs to the wall in the left-field corner. "They took all the vines down to tuck-point that wall, real gingerly, took a long time, laid 'em down. . . . We had to cover them in plastic, make sure nobody steps on 'em, and they retuck-pointed that wall, and we had to put them back up. . . . It was after the season, like October, November. We made sure they had to do it at that time because we had to get the vines back up to regrab."

The ivy gets trimmed at least 15 times a year, but the groundskeepers wait until the team leaves on a road trip because the job takes two days. In the mid-'90s, groundskeepers began using a scissors lift for the trimming job, Baird said. "Before that, it used to be with an old wooden ladder. Climb up the ladder, cut three feet, get off the ladder, move over three feet."

The groundskeepers take loving care of every inch of the ivy.

"The history of this field is those vines," Baird said. "We treat 'em like a baby."

THE BLEACHERS

It's the party room of Wrigley Field, where there's unreserved seating—and unreserved enthusiasm as well.

It's also where the strangest things happen. In 1920, the Cubs asked the police to break up gambling in the bleachers, and officers disguised themselves as sailors, ice wagon drivers, soldiers, and farmers and then raided the place, arresting 24 bettors. At least Wrigley Field has avoided the type of event that occurred in 1908 at the Cubs' previous home, the West Side Grounds, where a pregnant woman had her baby in the bleachers.

At Wrigley, the fans have given birth to their own traditions, such as throwing back opponents' home runs—a testimony of Cubs loyalty.

In the late '50s and early '60s, the bleachers were populated by a combination of teenage "greasers" in leather jackets and an organization called the Right Field

Wrigley's modern bleachers were built during the 1937 season. A pasteboard fence was thrown up between the outfield and the construction area. Legend has it that a batted ball hit a construction worker once, but if so, it probably occurred during batting practice, because construction work was supposed to stop at 2:30 P.M., half an hour before game time.

Bleacher Choir, a collection of friends, many from Chicago's North Shore suburbs, who would sing during the seventh-inning stretch. (This was before Harry Caray, of course.) The Bleacher Choir also carried out audacious plots to smuggle beer into the ballpark. Members claimed that they once had a guy sit in a wheelchair, with a pony keg hidden under a blanket, and wheeled him into the bleachers. They also boasted that they had lifted cases of beer by rope over the right-field wall. (Don't try this in the 21st century. Security is tighter.)

In the mid-'60s, the most famous bleacher group of them all appeared: the Bleacher Bums. The original Bums were 10 fans who sat in the left-field bleachers. Their name was coined when two fans, known as Ma Barker and Big Daddy from Morton Grove, held up a sign made out of a bedsheet with a hole in it that a fan stuck his head through. The sign read, "Hit the Bleacher Bum."

38

A bleacher tradition: throwing back visitors' home runs

A photo of the sign was widely published in newspapers, and the group was instantly famous.

"We *were* mostly bums—between college and high school, without jobs," recalled sports talk show host Mike Murphy, one of the original Bums, who was known as the "Mad Bugler" because he would blow a bugle that he'd picked up for $9 at a secondhand store.

The group's legend was expanded by a popular play, *Bleacher Bums*, written by Chicago's Organic Theater Company, including Joe Mantegna and Dennis Franz.

Among the stunts pulled by the real Bleacher Bums was tossing 12 mice into left field in an attempt to frighten the Cardinals' Lou Brock. The bums had heard that Brock had a mice phobia. Instead, Brock just laughed. But Willie Smith, playing left for the Cubs, was indeed afraid of mice, and he refused to take the field.

The basket was built to keep bleacher fans from jumping or falling onto the field. Now, occasionally, they fall into the basket.

Members of the grounds crew, carrying cardboard boxes, spent 10 minutes trying to round up the mice.

Tossing things onto the field used to be a common misdemeanor in the bleachers. In 1962, right-field fans pelted Dodgers rightfielder Frank Howard with peanuts, causing him to miss a fly ball. And sometimes, bleacher fans tossed themselves onto the field.

In 1970, Cubs management had finally had enough and built a wire basket at an angle atop the 11-foot-tall wall. The basket was designed mainly to keep fans from jumping or falling onto the field. But it also cut down on various types of fan interference, including fans throwing things onto the field, reaching over the wall, and draping their coats on the wall. (No longer would public-address announcer Pat Pieper declare: "Will the bleacher fans please remove their clothes.")

Even with the basket to separate them from the field, the bleacher fans stay close to the players.

Fans showered Hank "the Mayor of Wrigley Field" Sauer with bags of chewing tobacco after he hit a home run. (What he couldn't fit in his pockets he stashed in the vines.)

Billy Williams would play catch with young fans before the game. Andre Dawson got a respectful "salaam" from the right-field bleachers.

Former Cubs outfielder Rick Monday recalled, "There was one little group in right-center field that would be yelling and what have you. We had this thing going. I would motion one way and they would lean to the right, and I would motion another way and they would lean to the left, and another way and they'd stand up, and another way and they'd turn around. That was a group that was out there almost every day."

An usher looks for a home-run ball in the juniper bushes in center field, which form the hitter's background known as "the batter's eye." After the modern bleachers were built in 1937, straight center was filled with fans, many wearing white shirts or T-shirts, and players complained. The St. Louis Cardinals' Stan Musial said, "The background is just plain murder, and that's just what it's going to result in one of these days if something isn't done." In the late '40s, the Cubs experimented with a darkened Plexiglas atop the wall, but that didn't work. In 1952, the section was closed off for good (with the exception of the 1962 All-Star Game), and the Cubs later put up green tarpaulin and a plastic covering to improve the background. The juniper arrived in 1997.

Gary "Sarge" Matthews gave a military salute to the left-field bleacher fans and also passed out painter's caps with "Sarge" printed on them.

Wrigley Field's bleachers may be the most famous in sports. They're not simply "cheap seats"—they're a state of mind. Actually, these days, they're a state of mind with a split personality. There are the traditionalists, who follow the game closely and demand that opponents' home runs get thrown back, and there are the Mardi Gras types, such as fan Doug Weber, who said at a recent game, "It's one big party. If you're losing, you don't have to pay attention to the game."

Whether your eyes are trained on home plate or the blonde in the bikini top, the bleachers are fun in the sun.

THE SCOREBOARD

It's the biggest throwback in Wrigley Field: a scoreboard operated by hand, as if it were the scoreboard at the old-fashioned Little League park in your neighborhood.

When it was built under the direction of Bill Veeck as part of the 1937–38 renovation, it was state-of-the-art. Now, it's simply art, and primitive art at that.

Former Cubs official photographer George Brace, who died in 2002, always called it the "new scoreboard" because he remembered the old pre-1937 scoreboard, which featured two caricatures of ballplayers called the Wrigley "stick men"—with "stick" being a play on words, meaning both a baseball bat and a stick of Wrigley gum.

But whether it's old or new, the scoreboard at Wrigley Field is different. Most other major league ballparks have scoreboards that are, in effect, big-screen TV sets, featuring replays, pictures of fans, and even commercials. But the way Cubs fans see it, if they'd wanted to watch television, they would've stayed home. They came to Wrigley to see it all in person.

The scoreboard seems invulnerable, having never been hit by a baseball in a game. Two players came close—the Pirates' Roberto Clemente missing to the left

43

45

"In this day of computerized scoreboards and electronic message boards, Wrigley Field is still as refreshing as a pretty girl in a flimsy dress on a windy day."

—HALL OF FAME BROADCASTER
JIMMY DUDLEY

and the Cubs' Bill "Swish" Nicholson missing to the right. In a pregame stunt in 1951, golfer Sam Snead teed up a golf ball on home plate and hit the scoreboard.

One compromise to modern life is a small electronic message board that wishes happy birthday to fans, gives players' vital statistics, and announces upcoming game promotions. That went up in 1982.

But the line scores of the game at hand, and other games around the country, are done the way they always have been—by human beings putting up five-pound metal plates that are painted green, with the numbers in white or yellow.

The scoreboard is usually operated by three people, though it can have as many as five during weekends or at night, when many other games are taking place at the same time. The crew chief is Freddie Washington, a groundskeeper who sets

the foul lines before the games, then climbs up the ladder and enters the trapdoor into the 27-foot-high, 75-foot-wide scoreboard.

Inside, it's like being in the hull of a ship. It's all rust-colored paint atop metal, with bits of real rust poking out. When it rains, water forms in pools on the floor. There are few creature comforts—a rusty window fan hangs nearby for hot summer days. A box of Sterno cans is available to provide warmth on cold spring days. There are a mini-fridge and a water cooler and a plastic ice chest.

Freddie Washington puts up numbers right to left. "We have to think backward," he says.

The scoreboard has three levels inside, with Washington and an assistant on the first level, watching the game from the holes for the visitors' eighth inning, ninth inning, and total scores.

"This is the best seat in the house," Washington said. Indeed, it's such a vantage point that, according to 1950s Cubs pitcher Moe Drabowsky, the Cubs used to have their traveling secretary, Don Beebe, in the scoreboard stealing signs. If Beebe put his foot in the right-hand corner of a square, it would signal to the batter, 450 feet away, that the pitch was going to be a fastball.

Up one level from Washington's perch is Brian Helmus, known as the "Chairman of the Boards." Helmus is stationed at the ticker-tape machine, which prints

*"The Cubs have had two
problems: they put too few
runs on the scoreboard, and
the other guys put too many.
So what has the new
management announced
that it is improving? The
scoreboard."*

—COLUMNIST GEORGE F. WILL

48

out scores delivered by a service in Jersey City, New Jersey. He handles the posting of the scores for some games himself, with Washington and his assistant assigned to others. Helmus will call down to them: "Zero, top of the fifth, top game." The most important score, of course, is the game going on in front of them, and they have to pay close attention so they can update the hits and runs.

The balls, strikes, outs, and batter's number are controlled electronically from the press box by another groundskeeper-turned-scorekeeper, Rick Fuhs. The system, described in 1937 as embodying "ingenious new magnetic principles never before employed in scoreboard design," involves eyelets whose movement uncovers white dots that form numbers. When there's a question of whether a player has reached base on a hit or an error, Fuhs signals that, too, and Washington and crew can tell by the electronic buzz whether to add a hit to the team's total.

The scoreboard is both a boiler room and a shady perch. At the height of summer, it can be stifling. There's no air-conditioning, except the breeze created by the opening of vents on either end of the scoreboard. Which is not to say that it's always hot.

"I'll come up here in a coat even in the summertime," Washington said. "The Chicago wind is kind of crazy—it'll eat through your clothes like you don't have any clothes."

The "Chairman of the Boards," on level two, has a good view of any approaching thunderstorm—a better view, in fact, than anyone in the park, because most storms arrive from the west. When lightning starts, they leave. "Too much metal around this place," Washington said.

When the game ends, Washington has another duty. If the Cubs have won, he hoists the white flag with the *W* on it over the scoreboard. If they've lost, he hoists the blue flag with the *L*. (In the early years, before the Cubs used flags, Veeck put lights atop the scoreboard to notify elevated-train riders of a Cubs win or loss. Green meant victory. Red meant defeat.)

Before Washington leaves the ballpark, he also takes down the National League pennants atop the scoreboard, which have been put up in order of each team's divisional standing. Then the scoreboard goes to sleep.

The Wind

An invisible force haunts Wrigley Field, menacing pitchers, cheating hitters, and reminding fans that all manner of miracle might occur on any day, at any time.

The force is the wind, and it has defined Wrigley as baseball's most unpredictable park—a place where you might have both pitchers throw a no-hitter through nine innings (which happened in 1917) and a place where a record 26–23 slugfest might erupt (as it did in 1922, with 51 hits total and the Cubs defeating the Phillies). And it's not all ancient history: the Phillies got revenge on the Cubs, 23–22 in ten innings, in a 1979 game played on a warm, windy day. When the wind is blowing in, all pitchers can be Sandy Koufax; when the wind is blowing out, your second-string catcher becomes Johnny Bench.

Players and managers are devout believers in the Miracles of the Breeze.

In the magical year of 1984, Ryne Sandberg used to carpool with pitcher Rick Sutcliffe, catcher Jody Davis, and outfielder Keith Moreland. "When we were driving to the ballpark, first of all we'd check to see which way the wind was blowing," Sandberg said. "We had two or three flags we'd check every time when we drove down Irving Park Road. They were on some banks. As you got closer, then you really got an idea. We'd just check the flags and have a game plan."

"The wind is the 10th man on the field," said former Cubs manager Jim Lefebvre. "I saw [the Giants' Matt] Williams crush a ball that I knew was going to go at least 500 feet, and it wound up being a routine fly to shallow center field."

"Willie Mays used to say, 'There goes Ernie turning on his favorite windmill again.'"

—ERNIE BANKS

53

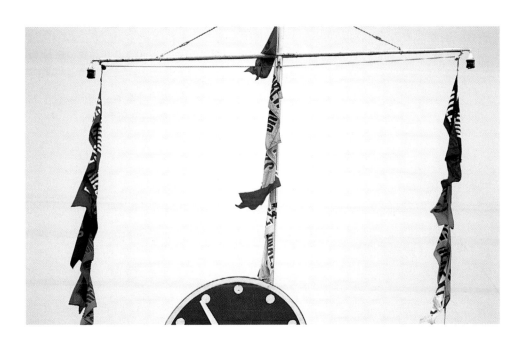

"It's intimidating to pitchers," said former star third baseman and current broadcaster Ron Santo. "I used to see pitchers come down to the end, look out, and they'd go, 'Ohhhh.' Whatever their game plan was, they knew they couldn't make a mistake, or bingo, it's gone."

Mitch Williams, the Cubs' closer in the late 1980s, was philosophical about it: "People make a big deal out of the wind blowing out. For the first two months of the season, you can't hit a ball out of there. It helps you as much as it hurts you. I think it evens out."

The Cubs have done their own count of wind conditions at the start of games at Wrigley Field. In five years, from 1996 through 2000, the wind was blowing in 58 percent of the time and blowing out 30 percent. There was a crosswind 12 percent of the time.

Wind isn't the only weather phenomenon to buffet Wrigley Field, and there's no retractable dome to activate when the rain comes. According to Chicago meteorologist Tom Skilling, a key factor in the ballpark's weather is its proximity to the lake—"That's a big part of the ball game right there."

An analysis by Tom Skilling, chief meteorologist for WGN-TV and the *Chicago Tribune*, shows that, early in the season, Wrigley's wind blows northeasterly (toward the southwest, straight in from center field). It averages 12 miles per hour in April, 11 m.p.h. in May, and 9 m.p.h. in June. In midsummer, the wind turns around and favors the hitters, blowing southwesterly (out to straight center)— 9 m.p.h. in July, 8 m.p.h. in August. In September and October, it's still a hitter's park, but it favors right-handed pull hitters because it's a southerly wind, blowing out to left field. For September, it's 9 m.p.h. The October wind, which the Cubs have rarely been lucky enough to experience, is 10 m.p.h. to left field.

The key factor is Wrigley's location, less than a mile from Lake Michigan. "Any time you've got a ballpark situated this close to a body of water, you're going to have frequent temperature variations, and that's the basis for wind," Skilling said.

The breeze can have a significant effect on a batted ball. Yale physics professor Robert K. Adair calculates that if a hit would travel 400 feet in a windless environment, it would go only 370 feet with a 10 m.p.h. breeze against it, and would go 430 feet with a 10 m.p.h. wind in its favor. At some ballparks, especially those with significant windbreaks in the outfield (such as double-deck outfield stands), the wind effect might be mitigated. But not at Wrigley. And there's another factor, too: Adair notes that Wrigley Field's altitude, 595 feet above sea level, is higher than Yankee Stadium's—enough so that a batted ball will travel five feet farther at Wrigley.

Given all those numbers, one would expect to see the home-run count skyrocket at Wrigley as the season progresses. But that's not what happens. Ed Hartig, a Cubs historian, reports that his figures for 1978–2000 show home runs per at-bats at Wrigley were actually higher in May (2.95 per 100) than in July (2.71) or August (2.83).

Which leaves the issue unsettled. Perhaps the wind factor is a myth, something for play-by-play broadcasters to talk about between pitches. After all, Chicago was nicknamed "the Windy City" not for its weather but for its boosterism and bluster. And while Chicago is gusty, it isn't America's windiest city—Boston and Kansas City have stiffer breezes.

Still, the players believe in the Wrigley winds, and who's to dispute them? Perhaps this is one case in which statistics lie, in which averages don't matter but incidents do—in which the unpredictability and ferocity of the wind create a lasting impression, and an uneasy anticipation, that anything can happen at any moment at Wrigley Field.

THE LIGHTS

Night baseball almost came to Wrigley Field in the same era when it arrived everywhere else. In December 1941, the Cubs had the steel for the towers on site and the lights on order, when World War II intervened.

"We had determined that we would put lights in, but then there was Pearl Harbor," said Jim Gallagher, the Cubs' general manager at the time. "Mr. Wrigley, the next morning, said, 'Cancel the order for lights.'"

The steel was donated to the war effort, and for the next 47 years, games at Wrigley would be under sunshine only, a practice that endeared the ballpark to the purists, if not to the team's accountants.

When major league games first began at night—at Cincinnati's Crosley Field in 1935—P. K. Wrigley called it "a passing fad." And he wasn't alone: *The Sporting News* declared in an editorial that "night baseball is just a step above dog racing." By 1948, when Tiger Stadium in Detroit lit up, every major league ballpark in America had baseball at night, except the one on the North Side of Chicago.

There were benefits to day-only baseball: a loyal following of housewives and schoolkids. But there was a downside, too: the 9-to-5 working crowd was shut out of the action.

Baseball theorists have managed to blame daytime baseball for the Cubs' late-season disappearing acts, especially in 1969. And that outlook survives to this day. In 2001, Cubs hitting coach Jeff Pentland said, "There has to be a reason Chicago hasn't won for a hundred years, and this is part of it. We're the last team that plays a lot of day games."

58

"Putting lights in Wrigley Field is like putting aluminum siding on the Sistine Chapel."

—NEWSPAPER COLUMNIST
ROGER SIMON

E. M. Swift, writing in *Sports Illustrated*, assaulted the daytime excuse: "This theory would be more acceptable if they were the Sahara Cubs and each player was stripped and bound in the sand before his turn at bat, but 2½ hours in the Chicago sun—half of which is spent in the dugout—could not seriously tax a fat albino."

William Shlensky, a 27-year-old holder of two shares of stock in the Cubs, sued P. K. Wrigley and other directors in 1966, seeking a court order forcing the installation of lights. Day-only baseball, the suit said, was "mismanagement and waste of corporation systems." Wrigley, of course, disagreed, openly expressing his concern about disturbing the sleep of the neighbors, and he prevailed in court.

The commitment to day-only baseball died with P. K. Wrigley. When Tribune Company took over in 1981, the lighting was on the wall.

*"Would it help the team to
have lights? Yes. We'd get
more rest."*

—SHORTSTOP LARRY BOWA

The Cubs' new general manager, Dallas Green, made clear his interest in installing lights—so clear, in fact, that organized opposition sprang up immediately and took the initiative, securing both city and state laws that effectively banned night games at Wrigley. The state law, passed in 1982, took the form of a "noise pollution" act, a notion that prompted pro-lights representative John F. Dunn to say, "Noise pollution at Wrigley can't be that much of a problem. There's nothing there to cheer about." The city ordinance, passed in 1983, allowed the Cubs to install lights—as long as they were turned off by 8 P.M.

The next season, the Cubs made the playoffs, and suddenly day baseball wasn't just a local issue. The networks didn't like broadcasting postseason games during the day. Before the 1985 season, Baseball Commissioner Peter Uebberoth sent the

62

Helicopters were used to help install the lights—six 33-foot light towers, each with 90 halide 1,500-watt bulbs designed to last three thousand hours.

Cubs a letter warning that future League Championship Series and World Series involving the Cubs might "be played elsewhere than at Wrigley Field, perhaps not even in Chicago," raising the ugly prospect of a Cubs World Series game taking place at St. Louis's Busch Stadium.

The next day, the Cubs filed suit challenging both the city and state laws because they applied only to Wrigley Field, but they lost in Cook County Circuit

Rick Sutcliffe throws the first pitch August 8, 1988, at Wrigley Field's first major league game under the lights.

Court. Judge Richard L. Curry's written opinion, on March 25, 1985, was a sometimes whimsical examination of the facts, laced with quotations from Jonathan Swift's *Gulliver's Travels* and Thomas Wolfe's *Of Time and the River*, as well as citing the poems "Tinker to Evers to Chance" and "Casey at the Bat." The ruling accused the Cubs of bad "scouting": "Everyone around the courthouse is familiar with 'Justice'—with her robes flowing, her blindfold and her scales. What the Cubs' 'book' on her failed to note is that she is a southpaw. Justice is a southpaw and the Cubs don't hit lefties!!!"

The Cubs weren't laughing, or if they were, they were thinking that they might just laugh all the way to a new stadium with lights in the northwest suburbs. It was time to play hardball. As Bernie Lincicome of the *Tribune* put it: "The Cubs are not the Cubs anymore, not the gentle souls who played in the sunshine as if their thumbs were on backwards."

The Cubs' consideration of leaving Wrigley Field in the mid-'80s might have been the ballpark's closest flirtation with death ever—or at least since the early '60s, when attendance was miserable. As the prospect of the ballpark's demise sunk in, the political mood shifted. Mayor Harold Washington signaled his support of lights. Although Washington's sudden death in 1987 put the issue on hold for a time, his successor, Eugene Sawyer, also gave the Cubs' plan the green light, with night games limited to 18, beer sales halted after 9:20 P.M., and fan parking prohibited on neighboring streets. The city council and the Illinois legislature lifted their bans, the Cubs put up their lights, and the first major league game at night in Wrigley Field was scheduled for August 8, 1988.

More than 1.5 million fans competed in a telephone lottery for 13,000 tickets. A longtime fan, Harry Grossman, age 92, pulled the switch that lit up Wrigley Field. The Chicago Symphony Orchestra played the National Anthem, and Ernie Banks and Billy Williams threw out ceremonial first pitches.

Banks recalled, "Me and Billy were standing there looking at the lights, and we said, 'I wish we were still playing.' Because the place looked so charming. It's a charming park day or night, but especially at night. It's like an actress without her makeup on in the daytime, but at night, wow!"

"Night baseball has a special quality. Because there are no lights in the outfield, it takes on a theatrical effect."

—Chicago architect
Philip Bess

65

Sluggers in the spotlight during a 1988 charity event to celebrate the new lights: (from left) Ernie Banks, Andre Dawson, Billy Williams, and Ryne Sandberg

The first night game wasn't as charming to everyone.

On the fourth pitch of the game, the Cubs' pitcher, Rick Sutcliffe, gave up a home run into the left-field bleachers by the Phillies' Phil Bradley.

And then it started raining. Television broadcaster Steve Stone said, "I remember doing a 2-hour, 45-minute rain delay in a tuxedo when it was a thousand degrees."

The game finally was called on account of rain, and the fans fled, including a woman who said as she left the park, "This proves that the Cubs are cursed."

Television talk show host David Letterman saw it this way: "The first time I tried it with the lights on, it was pretty much a washout, too."

The first official night game came the next day, with a 6–4 victory over the Mets, and night games have been a special and well-attended part of the Cubs' schedule ever since.

The players have made Wrigley Field famous,

but it takes more than a nine-man lineup

to put life in a legendary ballpark.

2 A CAST OF THOUSANDS

THE PLAYERS

Wrigley Field is an unpredictable place to play baseball, and that can be unnerving. When the wind is blowing out, the hitters love it. When it's blowing in, the pitchers love it. The lack of foul territory cheats pitchers out of foul-outs. The ivy can bedevil outfielders going after fly balls. The bullpens in foul territory make it perilous to go after foul balls.

It seems that all players have experienced some measure of hard luck at Wrigley Field.

"As a visiting pitcher, I appreciated it more when I wasn't starting that day," said Cubs broadcaster Steve Stone, who gave up a three-run homer to Billy Williams the first time he pitched at Wrigley.

Ken Holtzman, a fine pitcher for the Cubs in the '60s and '70s, once declared in a moment of pique: "I hate this ballpark. It stinks." Yet as a retiree, he returned to enjoy the park and sing "Take Me Out to the Ball Game."

The truth is, players love this park . . . after they retire.

Buck O'Neil (left), former Cubs coach and Negro Leagues legend, stands for the National Anthem with Billy Williams and Ernie Banks.

A caller to a sports radio station once called Wrigley Field "a historic land mine . . . I mean landmark." Some players, especially pitchers, might think the caller was right the first time. And the Cubs' World Series drought has encouraged the idea that the Cubs are a team benighted by freakish bad luck.

In 1920, when the Black Sox scandal erupted on the South Side of town, a Joliet man with a bad sense of direction walked up to the Cubs' Buck Herzog and slashed him with a knife, calling him "one of those crooked Chicago players."

The Cubs' Jose Cardenal once had to be scratched from the lineup because his left eyelid was stuck shut.

Pitcher Ray Fontenot once bruised his ribs when he tripped as he went to answer the bullpen phone.

Relief pitcher Jeff Fassero and his son Blake warm up before a game.

Slugger Dave Kingman once dislocated his shoulder while carrying his suitcase out of his hotel room.

Let's face it: broadcaster Jack Brickhouse had it right when he called the Cubs "the most unlucky team in sports."

But then again, they play in the most beautiful park in America, in front of the most forgiving, adoring fans around.

As slugger Andre Dawson put it, "To be afforded an opportunity to play in Wrigley Field, with the huge following nationwide, I don't think any player would turn his back on it."

And Wrigley Field has always welcomed colorful characters in uniform.

Even Moe Drabowsky, who used a bullpen phone to call a stockbroker during games in the late '50s.

Even the prickly Rogers Hornsby, who advised hitters: "Don't read. It'll hurt your eyes."

Even '70s hipster Joe Pepitone, a Cub who was the first major leaguer to use a hair dryer in the locker room.

Even drunken star Hack Wilson, described by sportswriter Warren Brown as "a high ball hitter on the field, and off it."

Even Lou Novikoff, who used to complain that the left-field foul line was crooked, and who once stole third with the bases loaded, explaining that he couldn't resist because he had gotten a "good jump."

"Wrigley is the best place. I never want to leave."

—Sammy Sosa

75

The top Cubs hitters of the '90s, one a master of contact, the other a captain of clout: Mark Grace and Sammy Sosa

Still talking strategy: Billy Williams and Ron Santo

"Every player should be accorded the privilege of at least one season with the Chicago Cubs. That's baseball as it should be played—in God's own sunshine. And that's really living."

—ALVIN DARK

77

Despite the challenges of playing at Wrigley, the players are a lot like the fans in their sense of awe when they experience their first game in the old ballpark.

Ron Santo recalled: "I'll never forget walking out of our dugout down there with Ernie Banks, onto the field, walking down to take batting practice. And I stepped onto the field—and I can see this, and it was so vivid in my mind, I don't know what it was, but there was so much electricity. It just moves you to another level . . . the electricity, the enthusiasm, and my whole career that's how I felt every time."

The players may have been unlucky on the field, but they've been lucky with the people in the grandstands, the box seats, and the bleachers. Retired Cubs players find themselves adored their entire lives.

"There's too much nature in that ballpark. You hit a pop-up one day and it's out of the park and hit a screaming mimi the next day and it stays in. That's a tough place to play half your games."

—FORMER CUBS CATCHER
HARRY CHITI

78

Pitcher Kyle Farnsworth takes an intentional walk with his dogs Strike (left) and Zeus.

"People say I was never with a winner," said Ernie Banks, "but what is a winner? I was indeed with a winner because I made lifetime friends on my ball club. I won every time I stepped onto the grass at Wrigley Field because I had such a wonderful relationship with the Cubs players, the fans, and all the people of Chicago, the greatest people in the world. Not on a winner? I was on a winner all my life."

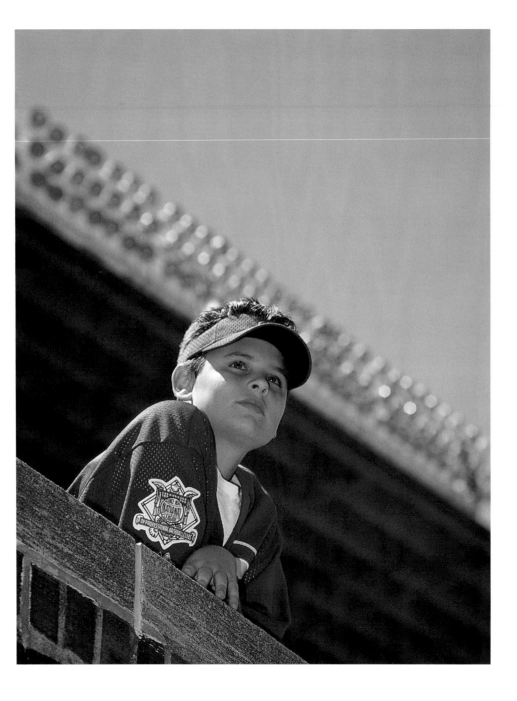

THE FANS

The faithful fans at Wrigley Field are a symbol of supreme patience. The last time the Cubs won a World Series, there was no federal income tax, the word *jazz* hadn't been invented, Charlie Chaplin hadn't made a movie yet, and women couldn't vote. And Wrigley Field hadn't been built.

That last World Series triumph was in 1908, and Cubs fans have suffered through nearly a century of frustration since. "Real Cub fans are 99.44 percent scar tissue," said columnist and fan George F. Will.

The Cubs didn't invent Ladies Day, but the team was the leading promoter of the idea for many decades.

"What makes the park so enjoyable is its human scale. It respects you as a fan and makes you a participant in the event."

—CHICAGO HISTORIAN
DOUG BUKOWSKI

82

Some people have viewed the team's weakness as the fans' strength.

"There's a different perspective at Wrigley Field—a clearer understanding of failure as a consistent part of baseball," wrote Roy Eisenhardt, Oakland A's president, in the *New Yorker* in 1986. "Because ball teams play every day, the chances for failure are always high, but the Cubs fans somehow understand that. It's a higher level of baseball culture."

And another good thing about being a Cubs fan: bonus viewing. "When you bought your ticket, you could bank on seeing the bottom of the ninth," said former Cub and TV personality Joe Garagiola.

Perhaps it's appropriate that the Cubs' marketing strategy under the Wrigleys was the same as the *Titanic*'s lifeboat policy: women and children first.

P. K. Wrigley popularized Ladies Day, a promotion that took place on Fridays generally, in which women who showed up at the gate were given free tickets (although, through the 1951 season, they were required to pay the tax). For a time in the '30s, the promotion was so popular that women had to write in for tickets and include a stamped, self-addressed envelope.

Wrigley's Ladies Days, and his insistence on keeping the park clean, ensured that women would come to Wrigley Field, and also that they would bring their children, creating another generation of Cubs fans.

Children have always been welcome at the park. In the '60s and earlier, kids coming home from school were allowed into the park free, through the Waveland Avenue entrance, after the seventh inning. The Cubs would also hire

children to collect trash in burlap sacks after the game. Their wage: a free pass to a future game.

Longtime Chicago broadcaster Bob Sirott recalled that when he was a kid, he and others used to pass peanuts from the front row into the third-base dugout to Ron Santo, who would look back at them with a wink.

Santo was always friendly to the fans. "I knew a lot of them by their first names," he said.

"The home-field advantage is when you see that this place is filled," Santo said. "It's like having a 26th man on your team. Because they're going to pump you up."

Former Cubs first baseman Mark Grace put it this way: "Having the people sitting so close to you at Wrigley creates a bond between the players and the fans

that you don't have anywhere else in the United States. First base is so close to the seats that I can hear people talking in the stands. It's like playing in a little town somewhere."

Don Dando, a season-ticket holder since the late '60s, has one of the best seats in the house—aisle 15, row 1, seat 1, right next to the Cubs' dugout on the third-base side.

"One time there was a third-strike call," Dando recalled, "and I went, 'Ohhhh!' rather loudly, and the umpire turned around and pointed to the Cubs' manager, Gene Michael, and threw him out of the game. Michael was bewildered, and he said, 'What did I do?' And the ump said, 'You were questioning the strike call.' People were looking at Michael and shaking their heads, and I was hoping they wouldn't turn around and single me out, and they didn't, you know. So I watch myself now. I got caught up in the moment."

Sometimes the players even welcome the fans' advice. Former Cubs pitcher Mike Krukow recalled, "Probably one of the most unique things about Wrigley Field—and I don't know if too many people ever talk about this—but it's probably one of the only places in the world where if a guy comes up in September, a hitter, and you don't know anything about him, you can sit down in the bullpen and ask the fans. They'll know. That's how good and knowledgeable they are about the game."

Which isn't to say that the players always are happy to get the fans' input.

In 1983, Cubs manager Lee Elia sabotaged his tenure by declaring, "Eighty-five

85

"If my colonel ordered me to take a hill, no matter what the cost in life and limb, I'd ask to bring five Cub fans along for the charge. From the very moment they're born, they know pain, suffering, danger, and misery."

—CUBS BROADCASTER
JACK BRICKHOUSE

86

percent of the people in this country work for a living, and the other 15 percent come out here and boo my players."

Hack Wilson, in the late '20s, found himself heckled by a fan named Edward Young (described by baseball writer Eddie Gold as "a milkman who had been drinking something other than milk"). After grounding out in the ninth inning, Wilson took a right turn, climbed into the stands, and punched out Young.

Such confrontations are rare, though player and fan frustration is inevitable when the Cubs tease their admirers the way they sometimes do—such as starting out 47–22 in 1977 and finishing with an 81–81 record. Or in 1999, when the Cubs were 32–23 but finished with a 67–95 mark.

That's when the fans' optimism is really tested. Still, many fans tend to think they're tantalizingly close to victory, if only the Cubs would make that one decisive move.

As longtime fan Jerry Pritikin once recalled, "My dad was in a coma for 30 days in 1980, and when he came out of it, his first words to me were, 'We gotta get rid of Kingman.'"

"I think of them as 35,000 of my best friends."

—FORMER CUBS PITCHER
RICK SUTCLIFFE,
COMPLIMENTING THE FANS

92

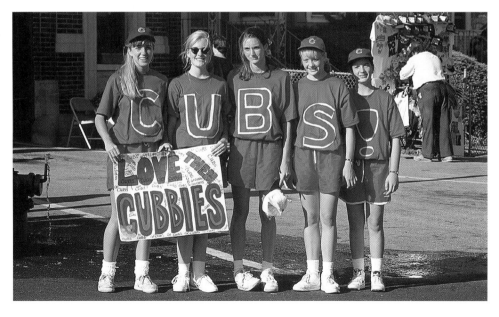

A Canada goose, one of many foreign tourists who visit Wrigley Field

THE NEIGHBORS

At some ballparks, the only next-door neighbors are parking attendants and acres of asphalt. Not so at Wrigley.

About 40,000 people live within a half mile, according to the local alderman, Bernie Hansen of the 44th Ward. Within a block of the ballpark, in addition to 40 bars and restaurants, are four car repair shops, three dry cleaners, three realty offices, two car washes, two Laundromats, two convenience stores, a hair salon, a nail salon, a lighting store, a window shade store, a video store, a firehouse, and a tarot card reader. The ballpark is indeed in the middle of a neighborhood.

The term *Wrigleyville* is common today, a tribute to the staying power of Wrigley Field. But that name for the neighborhood is fairly recent, made popular by real-estate agents in the '80s. "To me it will always be Lake View," said Hansen. In fact, Lake View was an independent township, with 275,000 residents, when it was annexed by the city of Chicago in 1889.

"Many years ago, it was mostly Scandinavian and German, and now it's everything. Probably 30, 40 different cultures and backgrounds," said Hansen.

The neighborhood was well connected to rail traffic, which is why Charles Weeghman wanted to build his ballpark there. Then, as now, some neighbors wanted the ballpark there, and some didn't. When Weeghman's plans were revealed, 700 local businessmen signed a petition of support. Neighborhood property owners sent their own petition—of disapproval—to Mayor Carter Harrison II.

The businessmen knew that the ballpark would bring people, and therefore would bring money. Wrigley Field was certainly good for nearby hot dog joints and, during Prohibition, a number of local speakeasies. But one of the most noticeable satellite busi-

nesses—the rooftops on Waveland and Sheffield Avenues—didn't begin in earnest until the Cubs became more successful and popular in the '80s. Before that, you might see a couple friends in folding chairs tending a Weber grill on one or two rooftops. But now, the rooftops have become entertainment centers, with manufactured grandstands on virtually every roof, catered food, indoor party rooms, big-screen televisions, and other amenities, all for $100 or more per person. The concept of the knothole gang—kids peeking through holes in the fence to watch the game—has been taken to a new, corporate extreme.

The lure of the rooftops was demonstrated in 1993 when Cincinnati Reds pitcher Tom Browning left the ballpark during a game to join a rooftop party on Sheffield. The Reds fined him $500.

Though the rooftop owners sometimes do not see eye-to-eye with the team owners, they do share a sense of optimism. Why else would Brixenivy, at 1044 West Waveland, tout its fireplace as "ideal for play-offs"?

One of the rooftops adjoins a longtime gathering spot, Murphy's Bleachers, at the corner of Waveland and Sheffield. Murphy's started out as a drive-up hot dog stand called Ernie's Bleachers in the '30s, then was JB's Bleachers for a few years, then became Ray's Bleachers in 1965 (the famed headquarters of the Bleacher Bums, run by Ray and Marge Meyer), and then, in 1980, became Murphy's Bleachers. Murphy's has always been a destination for pregame and postgame beverages, and when the team is out of town, it's a prime spot for watching the Cubs on television. Sharon Streicher, who was at Murphy's to watch the disastrous Game 5 of the 1984 National League playoffs televised from San Diego, uttered the legendary quote: "I went to the bathroom and it was 3–0. I came out and it was 6–3. I'm never going to the bathroom again."

For the people living around the ballpark, there are annoyances, even though the Cubs try to be a good neighbor, sending cleanup crews into the nearby streets after night games. Beyond the problems with noise and parking, Wrigley's neighbors must face the occasional baseball missile careening into their buildings.

In 1976, Dave Kingman, then playing for the New York Mets, smashed what was believed to be the longest home run at Wrigley up to that time. It traveled an

97

estimated 550 feet, bashing into a house on the east side of Kenmore Avenue, three houses down from the corner with Waveland. If the hit had gone three feet farther, it would have broken the window of Naomi Martinez's home and might have smashed the television on which she was watching the game.

Twenty years later, Sammy Sosa's game-winning home run broke a second-floor living-room storm window at 1034 Waveland, startling the apartment's tenant, a French immigrant named Philippe Guichoux, who had been reading a book in the kitchen. It was pure happenstance that Guichoux lived next to the ballpark. "I never watch baseball games," he said. "I don't have a TV."

In 2000, the Cubs' Glenallen Hill launched a rocket that reached the top of 1032 Waveland and was caught by fan Rick Frohock of Arlington Heights. It was believed to be the first time a home run had landed on a rooftop, and it may have been the most prodigious clout ever at Wrigley. (Home-run distances are not analyzed scientifically at Wrigley; they're estimates by public-address announcers Wayne Messmer and Paul Friedman, with advice from organist Gary Pressy, based on known comparable distances. Hill's hit was estimated at 490 feet, but an analysis commissioned by the *Chicago Sun-Times* found that the actual distance was 451.2 feet—with a potential for it to travel 600 feet if the building hadn't been there.)

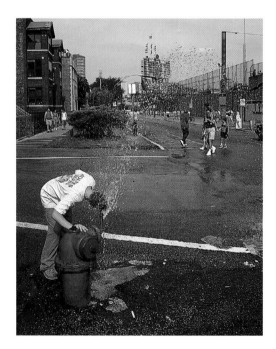

Anyone who gets hurt by flying baseballs can get medical attention at a beautiful brick firehouse built in 1915 beyond the left-field grandstand. The firefighters there are big Cubs fans, and in 1984 they put up an overly optimistic sign that read, "Official firehouse of the '84 World Series."

99

"Back in '85," recalled firefighter John Sampson, "they asked us not to put it up [again] because a lot of the players said it jinxed 'em."

When not answering emergency calls, the firefighters follow the Cubs on television, enjoying what they call "surround sound"—the sound from the TV and the crowd noise outside. In 1984, a foul ball hit by Ron Cey found its way to the firehouse. "He hit one that must have ricocheted at one point into the kitchen," Sampson said. "We were watching it on TV and said, 'Damn, let me see if this one could . . .' and all of a sudden it just rolled right in."

*"Any employee wishing to
miss work because of death
or serious illness please
notify the office by 11 A.M.
on the day of the game."*

—SIGN IN A RESTAURANT NEAR
WRIGLEY FIELD

102

A marriage made in heaven, or near it: while the game is going on, a wedding takes place on a rooftop on Sheffield.

The Lakeview Baseball Club at 3633 North Sheffield displays its enigmatic sign, which was put up in April 1996. *Eamus catuli* means "Let's go Cubs" in Latin. (Actually, *catuli* means "whelps," young offspring of a dog, wolf, bear, lion, seal, etc., which is the closest Latin word to "cubs.") The AC stands for *anno catuli* and measures the year in "Cubs time": the first two digits are the number of years since the Cubs won their division, the middle two digits are the number of years since they won a National League pennant, and the last two digits are the number of years since the Cubs won the World Series.

106

THE BALLHAWKS

A scavenger army is encamped on Waveland Avenue outside the ballpark. Some people are there for a few minutes or a few innings. Some are there for decades.

Eight or 10 diehards, most of them middle-aged, are there virtually every day, with their baseball gloves at the ready, their ears trained to the radio play-by-play, and their eyes gazing over the left-field wall, toward home plate. The diehards go after balls during spring training and at other ballparks such as Miller Park in Milwaukee and Comiskey Park on the South Side. Sometimes they're in the bleachers. But mostly, these days, they're outside Wrigley Field, on Waveland Avenue. They often work off-hours jobs so they can be there at game time.

The ballhawks keep personal statistics. They know how many batting-practice balls they've caught, how many home runs in actual games, how many grand slams.

Gary "Moe" Mullins is the ballhawks' Hank Aaron, the career leader. He's snagged more than 3,600. The ballhawks' version of Barry Bonds is Dave Davison, whose 199 balls in 1999 is the season record. Their rivalry is a friendly one. Mullins jokes about Davison: "He's the baddest, meanest, knock-over-kids-est guy out here."

Fans on Waveland display the flag of the Dominican Republic in honor of native son Sammy Sosa.

"It's great for me, knowing they're waiting outside for me to hit a home run. Every time I hit it, I remember that they're waiting for this ball."

—SAMMY SOSA, ON THE BALLHAWKS

112

On weekends or during important games, the diehards are joined by scores or even hundreds of tourist-type, would-be ballhawks, whom the diehards refer to disparagingly as "passerbys."

The ballhawk crowd was at its peak in the ninth inning on September 13, 1998, during the home-run race between the Cardinals' Mark McGwire and the Cubs' Sammy Sosa. McGwire had already broken Roger Maris's record of 61 in a season, and Sosa had hit his 61st earlier in the game. Sosa cranked home-run number 62, which sailed over the left-field bleachers and landed in the alley off Waveland between Kenmore and Sheffield. It was a crazy scene—ballhawks young and old scrambled around babies in strollers to go after the ball. As if written in a script, all-time great ballhawk Mullins was the one who managed to grab Sosa's ball, but then he got crushed in a wild pileup of bodies. It was a scene so bizarre that only a term from a foreign sport—the word *scrum* from rugby—could describe it. A man in the crowd, Mike Steinbacher, recalled: "I was in the scrum and came out unscarred, which was a victory for me. It got a little crazy. A guy in a wheelchair got flipped over in the mayhem."

Out of the tangle of humanity, with the ball in hand, came suburban mortgage broker Brendan Cunningham—a classic "passerby," according to the veterans. Mullins protested that the ball had been pried out of his hand. Cunningham got a police escort from the scene and declared that he would sell the ball to finance his child's college education. Mullins filed suit against Cunningham and got a temporary restraining order blocking him from selling the ball or giving it to Sosa. Eventually, Mullins dropped the suit when they agreed to give the ball back to Sosa.

"I got torn ligaments. I got lifetime scars."

—BALLHAWK GARY "MOE" MULLINS, DESCRIBING THE STRUGGLE OVER SAMMY SOSA'S 62ND HOME-RUN BALL IN 1998

114

Despite legal reversals, despite advancing age, despite blazing heat or chilling rain, the ballhawks keep coming out.

Rich Buhrke, in his mid-fifties, has spent more than 40 years as a ballhawk. He's caught more than 3,200 balls, many of which he's donated to Little Leagues.

But why is a grown man standing on a Waveland Avenue sidewalk with a base-ball glove on his hand, wearing headphones tuned to the radio, his eyes trained toward the ballpark? Why does he keep coming day after day?

"It's the last grasp of my youth," said Buhrke. "Some say it's the last grasp of my sanity."

THE BROADCASTERS

At Wrigley Field, you don't have to play to be famous. All you have to do is play-by-play. Harry Caray was more well known than the players, and Jack Brickhouse is so fondly remembered that his trademark phrase "Hey-hey!" is on the ballpark's foul poles.

Four Cubs announcers have reached the Baseball Hall of Fame: Caray, Brickhouse, Milo Hamilton, and Bob Elson, "the Old Commander," who was the voice of the Cubs in the '30s and covered the White Sox for a longer hitch.

The first radio broadcast of a Cubs game at Wrigley Field occurred October 1, 1924, when WGN's Sen Kaney announced a city series exhibition game against the White Sox. The first major league game at Wrigley was broadcast April 14, 1925, on WGN, with Quin Ryan at the mike atop the grandstand roof calling an 8–2 Cubs victory over Pittsburgh.

Jack Brickhouse created an air of excitement even when there wasn't much on the field to cheer about.

"No doubt about it!"

—LOU BOUDREAU

Radio stations were eager to broadcast live events, and Wrigley Field was very much alive. In the '20s, at least five stations were broadcasting the Cubs.

Television came into the picture after World War II, with Whispering Joe Wilson calling the shots on WBKB-TV beginning in 1946. (He was known as "Whispering Joe" because of his stage-whisper style while calling bowling tournaments.) WGN launched its five-decades-and-counting television run in 1948, with Brickhouse at the mike. At the time, there was no national network programming to fill the airtime, and the Cubs filled the void. By 1949, WENR joined the fun, with Rogers Hornsby doing the play-by-play, and three television stations were broadcasting the Cubs simultaneously. There were afternoons in Chicago when there was nothing but Wrigley Field on the TV screen.

116

Bob Elson, a lunch pal of Baseball Commissioner Kenesaw Mountain Landis, was tapped by Landis to call a dozen World Series, including the 1932 "Called Shot" game in which Babe Ruth vanquished the Cubs.

The two giants of Cubs broadcasting, Jack Brickhouse and Harry Caray, stand on the Cubs'
Walk of Fame.

"Back, back, back, back.
That's it. Hey-hey!
Hey-hey!"

—JACK BRICKHOUSE

117

"Phil Wrigley wanted as much television exposure as he could get," said Arne
Harris, who was senior producer-director of WGN Sports. "Most people in sports
thought it would hurt, with people staying home. But Mr. Wrigley thought television would create new fans, especially women."

The Cubs became, as Harris put it, "the longest-running daytime soap opera
in history" and "the only daytime show without a doctor in it."

It became the team beloved by housewives and schoolkids.

"You'd be amazed at the number of people who come up to me and say when
they were kids they rushed home from school to watch the Cubs' game," said
Harris.

"I don't care who wins, as long as it's the Cubs."

—BERT WILSON

WGN ballyhooed its "advanced" TV cameras with a three-foot-long "zoomar" lens.

The marathon man of Cubs broadcasting was Brickhouse, the play-by-play man on WGN-TV from 1948 to 1981. Brickhouse also called White Sox home games for three decades. As the *Chicago Tribune*'s Steve Daley once put it, "Jack Brickhouse has seen more bad baseball than any person, living or dead." Brick-house, whose voice was the first ever heard on WGN-TV, stayed busy during foot-ball season, too, calling the Bears' games with *Chicago Sun-Times* columnist Irv Kupcinet.

Brickhouse was a member of the Cubs' board of directors and was a dogged promoter of Cubs baseball for decades. "That's the challenge that made Brickhouse so good—that he never or seldom had a winning club," said veteran Chicago broadcaster Red Mottlow.

"He had a great facility for storytelling," Mottlow said.

"He was the only guy I ever met who didn't mind rain delays," Harris recalled. "He loved to talk."

One of the most respected Cubs broadcasters was WGN Radio's Jack Quinlan, who was killed in a car accident at spring training in Arizona in 1965, cutting short a promising career. Many contemporaries were certain that Quinlan was headed for the top ranks of sports broadcasting on the national level. Certainly,

Quinlan's eulogy, by WGN's Jack Rosenberg, was an inspired tribute: "His voice possessed the firmness of a hearty handshake. The resonance of a finely tuned harp. The clarity of a starry night. The quality of a prayer."

But all Cubs broadcasters, even the venerable Brickhouse, were overshadowed by the sensation that was Harry Caray.

Soon after the Tribune Company bought the Cubs in 1981, it made a brilliant business decision: hiring Caray. The former play-by-play man for the St. Louis Cardinals, Oakland A's, and Chicago White Sox had a fun-loving style, an affinity for the fans, a refreshing honesty, and a knack for making a simple baseball game into a momentous event. And he popularized the singing of "Take Me Out to the Ball Game" during the seventh-inning stretch, a tradition that attracted fans to the park and kept them there.

"They could be losing 15–0 and people would not leave that ballpark until they'd sung that song," Harris said.

Current Cubs TV announcer Chip Caray said of his grandfather, "He brought the magic and majesty of Wrigley Field to a nationwide audience because of the

"Don't worry about foul balls, Mr. President—I'll protect you."

—Harry Caray to
Ronald Reagan

121

When President Ronald Reagan did an inning of play-by-play with Caray near the end of his term in 1988, he said, "You know, in a very few months, I'm going to be out of work, so I thought I ought to audition."

"Holy mackerel!"

—VINCE LLOYD

cable superstation, WGN. . . . People who'd never been to Wrigley Field and Chicago saw this place, saw 30,000 people in it every single day."

Harry Caray was open to the public, even leaving his phone number listed.

To him, it was simple: "The fans aren't looking for a Pavarotti or some golden-throated tenor from the Metropolitan Opera. They accept me because I talk like

Arne Harris, shown inside the WGN production truck, directed a crew of twenty, including seven people operating the cameras.

Radio play-by-play man Pat Hughes

"Get out the tape measure!
It's gone!"

—PAT HUGHES

a fan, and react like a fan. These are my people, and we talk the same language—baseball."

Caray and the superstation took the Cubs to marketing nirvana, creating fans throughout the country. Locally, Caray was an instant legend in Chicago bars and restaurants, known for his after-hours conviviality. He seemed to know every bartender, maître d', and waiter in Chicago, and before long, he was appointed "the mayor of Rush Street."

Caray wasn't exactly a textbook announcer, and as he got older, his malapropisms and misstatements became legend. He would say, for example, "Mike Marshall just got back from Los Angeles, where he was getting cocaine for his injured foot." And then partner Steve Stone would politely correct him, "That's novocaine, Harry."

Chip Caray and Steve Stone work through a rain delay.

Such mistakes didn't seem to dim Caray's luster, and people who couldn't name a single player knew who was doing the play-by-play.

Former Cubs manager Jim Frey said, "In 1984, if I walked down the street with Harry Caray, Ryne Sandberg, and Rick Sutcliffe, nine out of ten people would say, 'Hi, Harry.'"

Despite all the hoopla, Caray always remembered that the game was the main event. When he returned after his stroke in 1987, he got a surprise phone call from

President Ronald Reagan on the air in the early innings of a game. After a brief conversation, Caray abruptly cut off the president, saying, "Excuse me, Mr. President, but Bobby Dernier just got a bunt single, and I gotta get back to the baseball game." Then Caray hung up on the president of the United States. The Cubs were more important.

According to Stone, the fans help the broadcasters realize how special Wrigley Field is.

"It was a place of business to us," said Stone. "But almost every day, we would run into fans who were seeing this place for the first time and were seeing it with this sense of awe that everyone has when they're seeing it for the first time. That reminded us just how special this place was."

"It might be, it could be, it is! Holy cow!"

—Harry Caray

A crowd of 50,187 fans watches the Bears beat the Los Angeles Rams 24–3 in 1955.

The Cubs are the permanent residents of Wrigley Field,

but others have been temporary boarders,

including the Bears, rodeo riders, wrestlers, jugglers, ski jumpers,

and even presidents of the United States.

3   SIDESHOWS

The Bears

They are the most successful home team ever to play at Wrigley Field.

In their five decades at Wrigley, 1920–70, the Bears won eight titles, including four title-game victories at Clark and Addison—in '33, '41, '43, and '63.

The total might've been five, except the 1932 championship game had to be moved out of icebound Wrigley Field and played indoors at Chicago Stadium. The Bears defeated the Portsmouth, Ohio, Spartans on an 80-yard field. To compensate for the shorter playing area indoors, every time a team crossed midfield, it was penalized 20 yards.

When the Bears first played at Wrigley Field, they were called the Decatur Staleys, and they were the visiting team, going up against the hometown Chicago Tigers. The Staleys were sponsored by A. E. Staley, owner of a downstate corn products company, and were run by George Halas, a native of a Bohemian neighborhood on Chicago's Near South Side, and his partner, Ed "Dutch" Sternaman.

128

The Staleys played twice against the Tigers at Wrigley Field in 1920, and then visited the ballpark a third time for the title game against the Akron Pros (also known as the Indians), which ended in a 0–0 tie. That third time, Wrigley Field was a neutral site, but the next year, 1921, it became the Bears' den. That was when Staley let Halas and Sternaman take over the team and bring it to the big city. The Chicago Staleys reached a deal with Cubs executive William Veeck Sr. to play at Wrigley: the Cubs would get 15 percent of gross receipts for use of the stadium, unless receipts exceeded $10,000, in which case the rate would rise to 20 percent. The Cubs would get concession receipts, and the Bears would pocket scorecard revenues.

At first, the gridiron at Wrigley Field ran east-west, along the first-base line. But for most of the Bears' stay, the field was north-south, stretching from the first-base dugout to the left-field wall.

In either configuration, a football field was a tight fit. Wide receivers (or split ends, as they were known then) would sometimes catch a pass in the end zone and step into the baseball dugout before they could slow down.

Halas recalled running back Bronko Nagurski's encounter with the cramped conditions in 1930: "The Bears were on about the two-yard line. Nagurski got the handoff. With head down and legs churning, he plunged into the line. Nagurski blasted through two would-be tacklers as though they were a pair of old saloon doors and kept on going right through the end zone. His head still down, Nagurski ran full speed into the brick outfield wall there at Wrigley Field. He went down, then got up and trotted off the field. As he approached me on the sideline, he shook his head and said, 'That last guy really gave me a good lick, coach.'"

The team was called the Chicago Staleys for only one year. Then they became the Chicago Bears. Halas considered naming his team the Cubs but then realized that "football players are bigger than baseball players, so if baseball players are Cubs, then certainly football players are Bears."

Halas was a player-coach and a standout in both roles. During a rainy game at Wrigley Field against the Oorang Indians in 1923, he picked up a fumble by Jim Thorpe and returned it 98 yards for a touchdown, an NFL record that stood for 49 years.

But Halas, who bought out Sternaman and took full ownership in 1933, made his real mark as a coaching innovator. He was the first to hold daily practices, to establish a preseason training camp, to place a coach in the press box, and to study game film. And, of course, his innovations with the T formation and the man in motion revolutionized the NFL. Even in groundskeeping he was a pioneer, developing a method of protecting the playing field by laying out tarpaulin.

The Bears' first Wrigley Field sellout was Thanksgiving Day, 1925. It was Red Grange's first game as a Bear, a 0–0 tie against the Chicago Cardinals before 36,000 fans. (It's amazing that the early NFL ever became popular, with all those scoreless ties.)

"Halas will sell a ticket anywhere he can put a chair. Many's the time a player has come out of the game and found some guy in his seat on the bench—and usually the guy has a ticket stub for it."

—DALLAS COWBOYS GENERAL
MANAGER TEX SCHRAMM

129

Halas was always looking to increase Wrigley Field's capacity, and in 1948 he installed a 50-row section of temporary bleachers in the outfield to boost seating by 10,000. He also put field seats along the sidelines and end zones, and he sold several thousand standing-room tickets when there was demand. "The fans were at our elbow," Halas recalled. At its height, football capacity at Wrigley was more than 50,000.

"Wrigley Field was an interesting place for football," said broadcaster Jack Brickhouse. Because of the temporary bleachers, Brickhouse noted, "Wrigley Field had more seats between the goal lines than either Soldier Field or Yankee Stadium."

The Bears used to practice at Wrigley Field, too, but not without a certain amount of paranoia. According to player Don Kindt, during practices in the '40s and '50s, Halas would have trainer Andy Lotshaw and others walk around the upper deck to see whether they could spot any spies in the apartment buildings that overlooked the ballpark. No espionage agents were ever caught.

The baseball park was home to many of the Bears' all-time greats, including Nagurski, Grange, and the toughest linebacker of them all, Dick Butkus, who once declared matter-of-factly, "I wouldn't ever set out to hurt anybody deliberately unless it was, you know, like in a league game or something." Another star was running back Gale Sayers, who may have had the finest single football performance ever at Wrigley Field, with a record-tying six-touchdown day in 1965 against the San Francisco 49ers.

But by the end of the '60s, the Bears were outgrowing Wrigley Field. The NFL had set a minimum-capacity rule; Wrigley was simply too small to host pro football.

To Halas, the move to Soldier Field was inevitable: "The baseball season was so long that we had to play all of our preseason and two or three regular games out of town."

Still, it was a great run at Clark and Addison, where the Bears' winning percentage was over .700. Wrigley Field hasn't hosted a pro football game since 1970, but it apparently still holds an NFL record as the scene of more regular-season and

postseason games than any other stadium in league history. The Pro Football Hall of Fame keeps no official records on the subject, but Wrigley hosted at least 359 NFL games—five with the Chicago Tigers as home team in the early '20s, at least 30 with the Chicago Cardinals hosting, at least 323 with the Bears as home team, and the 1920 championship game. Cleveland's now-demolished Municipal Stadium is close behind, with 342 NFL games hosted. Giants Stadium at the Meadowlands in New Jersey is coming up fast, because it hosts both the Giants and Jets, and is on pace to pass Wrigley Field sometime in this decade.

132

Three cold and tired Bears on Thanksgiving Day, 1925: (from left) George Halas, Bill Fleckenstein, and Red Grange

Wrigley is a fond memory for many Bears. "I played in both Wrigley Field and Soldier Field with the Bears," Sayers recalled, "and I must admit I really enjoyed Wrigley Field. You definitely had a home-field advantage in Wrigley Field, unlike Soldier Field, where the people in the stands are so far away from the field. Wrigley Field being a baseball stadium, the fans were right on top of you, behind you, behind the benches. They were close and they were loud, and all the other teams sure knew they were in Bear territory."

THE ETCETERAS

Events at Wrigley Field have included circus acts, a rodeo, and even a ski-jumping contest. The ballpark's owners didn't leap to the inevitable conclusion that the park should be a baseball park exclusively. They tried plenty of other things in addition to baseball.

In fact, there were lights at Wrigley Field even before there were Cubs in Wrigley Field, and even before it was called Wrigley Field.

In June 1915, "Lucky Charlie" Weeghman held "first-class hippodrome acts" at the park at night while the Chicago Whales were playing out of town. An admission fee ranging from 10 to 30 cents was charged to view such circus-style performers as "The Five Juggling Normans" and "the great base ball pantomime comedian George Slivers." (Yes, *baseball* was two words back then.) As the *Sporting Life* weekly newspaper described it, "A complete lighting system has been installed, and the double spotlight system will be used."

Over the next four decades, Wrigley Field hosted a number of special events, both during the day and at night. After the upper deck was built in the '20s, the Cubs installed six banks of floodlights on the roof, and they often set up additional portable lights at field level. Such a system wasn't nearly bright enough to make night baseball feasible, but it was tolerable for such events as the September 1934 battle between Jim Londos and Ed "Strangler" Lewis for the world wrestling championship, at which a crowd of 35,265 witnessed Londos's triumph.

"We had to surrender our lockers to the Bears. We had to get out of their way. We didn't want to mess it up by getting in the World Series."

—ERNIE BANKS

133

"Sgt. Torger Tokle won the Norge Ski Club jump in Chicago with a leap of only 89 feet. The slide was built into the second deck of Wrigley Field and wasn't long enough for the usual distance."

—The Stars and Stripes, 1944

134

Bovine comedy: a cow-milking contest before a Cubs game

Boxing was popular at Wrigley in the mid-'40s, and among the palookas taking part was middleweight Jake LaMotta, a punching bag who became far more famous 40 years later when the film *Raging Bull* came out. LaMotta duked it out with Chicago lightweight Bob Satterfield under the lights in a ring over home plate. Like a lot of Cubs before and after, Satterfield was called out at home in the seventh.

In that same era, in January 1944, a ski ramp was installed in the ballpark for an invitational tournament run by the Norge Ski Club (pronounced Nor-gee, with a hard *g*). The ramp began in the upper deck, with skiers landing around second base. A local company provided ice that was crushed to make the ramp slick. A crowd of 6,387 attended.

"It was kind of silly," said Jim Gallagher, who was Cubs general manager at the time. "But it was a way to use the ballpark and take in a little bit of money."

At the time, Gallagher recalled, people didn't want to travel, because of gas rationing and other World War II conditions, and the Wrigley ski jump allowed them to enjoy winter sports without traveling outside Chicago to their usual facilities.

Even basketball has been played at Wrigley Field. On August 21, 1954, Abe Saperstein's Harlem Globetrotters beat the George Mikan All-Stars 57–51 before

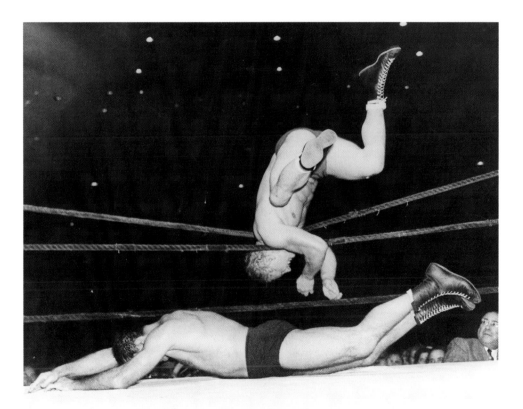

Wrestling at Wrigley: Buddy "Nature Boy" Rogers is roped in by Lou Thesz in 1950.

Members of the All-American Girls Professional Baseball League and Red Cross workers pose with Cubs rookie catcher Dewey Williams to promote Red Cross festivities at Wrigley Field in July 1944, featuring a doubleheader by the women's league.

a crowd of 14,124. The game was played under the lights, on a portable plywood court laid on top of the infield.

Chuck Holton, a member of the Globetrotters at the time, recalled, "The lighting was not great, but it sufficed."

The floor had some dead spots, but it was better than some floors the Globetrotters had performed on during their European tour in previous months, Holton said. "We were used to playing on odd surfaces like bullrings—that was even worse—and on open fields in Europe."

Rodeo came to Wrigley in 1946, '47, and '52. Alderman Bernie Hansen of the 44th Ward recalls watching the bronco riding and steer wrestling as a child.

"Sid the bull was the big attraction," Hansen said. "Somebody was going to ride on Sid the bull. He was the most notorious bucking bull around at the time. My uncle Ray Culver tried to ride Sid the bull, broke his arm."

DePaul University played some of its home football games at Wrigley Field until the late '30s, when the school abandoned football as a varsity sport. And in the late '70s and early '80s, the Chicago Sting soccer team played at Wrigley Field when it didn't have use of Soldier Field or Comiskey Park.

The ballpark has been host to nonsporting events as well, including religious conventions by the Jehovah's Witnesses, who left the park cleaner than when they'd arrived. In 1948, a political rally was held there, too, and—appropriately for the Cubs—the candidate was an also-ran, Progressive Party presidential hopeful Henry Wallace.

Not all the baseball at Wrigley has been major league action. In 1920, Wrigley hosted a high school game between the New York School of Commerce and Chicago's Lane Tech, and a shy junior named Lou Gehrig hit a home run out of the park to spark a 12–8 victory for the visitors.

The Negro Leagues' Satchel Paige brought a black all-star team to Wrigley Field in May 1942, and it defeated the Dizzy Dean All-Stars 3–1 before a crowd of 29,000. The teams planned to play at Wrigley again on July 4, but Baseball Commissioner Kenesaw Mountain Landis put the kibosh on the game because Satchel and Diz were outdrawing major league teams.

The All-American Girls Professional Baseball League played exhibition games at Wrigley in the 1940s. The league, which was featured in the 1992 film *A League of Their Own*, was enthusiastically supported by P. K. Wrigley and his wife, Helen. In fact, Mrs. Wrigley helped design the skirts and satin shorts that made up the uniforms for the league, which operated from 1943 through 1954. Appropriately, the moviemakers used Wrigley Field as one of their locations, because the park had changed so little from the '40s.

The women's league's all-star game, played at Wrigley Field on July 1, 1943, under temporary lights, is sometimes referred to as the first night baseball game at Wrigley, but the game was more like softball than baseball. The women used a 12-inch ball, and their league didn't allow overhand pitching until 1948. (What could

The Chicago Sting soccer team played part of its schedule at Wrigley Field in the late '70s and early '80s.

be considered the first night baseball game at Wrigley occurred a week earlier, without lights, when the Cubs and Cardinals played a game that started at 6 P.M. and ended at 8:17.)

These days, not much other than Cubs baseball happens at Wrigley Field. But some people still have ideas.

Alderman Hansen said, "I suggested that they do a Chicagoland winter ice follies in the outfield in the off-season, use the ballpark year-round, and to erect a slide from the scoreboard down into second base. You know how many people would pay five bucks to climb up in that scoreboard and take a slide down into second base?"

THE CELEBRITIES

The famous have always flocked to Wrigley Field, to throw out the first pitch, to sing "Take Me Out to the Ball Game," to bask in the crowd at Clark and Addison.

The ballpark has hosted presidents, foreign dignitaries, religious leaders, singers, movie stars, and even gangsters.

Two of the ballpark's biggest fans were political opposites: Republican icon Ronald Reagan and Democratic stalwart Hillary Rodham Clinton.

Reagan, before he became a movie star and the 40th president of the United States, was a broadcaster at WHO radio in Des Moines, doing re-creations of Cubs games.

"I was making it sound like on-the-spot reporting, with Western Union ticker tape from Wrigley Field while the Cubs were battling for the 1938 pennant," Reagan recalled. "Billy Jurges was at bat when the telegraph wire went dead. Rather than switch to music and lose the audience, I had Jurges foul off some pitches. Then I described a deep foul that just missed being a homer and the fight between two kids going for the ball. It had to be the longest at-bat in history. Finally, the ticker started again. I had to laugh because it turned out Jurges had popped up on the first pitch."

139

In fact, the Cubs helped make Reagan a movie star. While in southern California covering the team's spring training for WHO, Reagan met the Hollywood agent who got him his first big break.

During his surprise visit to Wrigley Field on September 30, 1988, Reagan threw out the first pitch. The conservative's toss was "to the right," an aide noted. Then Reagan did an inning of play-by-play with Harry Caray, in which he referred to the Cubs as "we."

Reagan was the first president to visit Wrigley Field. (Franklin D. Roosevelt was in the ballpark for Game 3 of the 1932 World Series—the "Called Shot" game—but that occurred a month before FDR was elected president.)

Senator Hillary Clinton's connections to the Cubs go deep. She grew up in suburban Park Ridge. "When I was young, I came here with my dad," she said. "Then, when I was older, I came here with friends. Coming to the ballpark in those days was really a big deal."

After she became First Lady, she was invited to throw out the first pitch. That prompted *Los Angeles Times* columnist Mike Downey to quip: "Knowing the Cubs, she'll probably hurt her arm."

Her visit in April 1994 was greeted by a smattering of boos, as are many politicians' appearances at ballparks. A light plane with a sign reading, "Hillary, U have the right to remain silent" flew by, referring to the then-ongoing Whitewater investigation. But Clinton rose above it, autographing baseballs "H. R. Clinton" and singing "Take Me Out to the Ball Game" with Harry Caray.

Her husband made his own lower-profile visit to Wrigley a few years later, enjoying the game from a skybox where bulletproof glass had been installed.

One of the most memorable celebrity visits was by actor and comedian Bill Murray, who grew up in the Chicago area as a Cubs fan. When Harry Caray had a stroke in 1987, a series of guest television announcers were brought in, including Murray, who didn't bother to hide his disgust for the visiting Montreal Expos:

"[Tim] Wallach's under it and makes the catch," Murray said. "Too bad he didn't fall."

140

Senator Hillary Rodham Clinton grew up as a Cubs fan in suburban Park Ridge.

142

Walter Payton arrived a few years too late to play football at Wrigley, but he didn't fumble his chance to throw out the first pitch at a baseball game.

At least two guys named Dizzy have performed at Wrigley Field: pitcher Dizzy Dean and horn player Dizzy Gillespie.

When the Cubs' Chico Walker took a mighty swing and missed, Murray said, "He was trying to tie up this game with one swing of the bat, which isn't easy when your team is winning 7–0."

At game's end, Cubs broadcaster Steve Stone told him, "Bill, I think you've revolutionized play-by-play."

As the ballpark becomes more of a novelty, more celebrities are making pilgrimages.

On any day, fans might share the ballpark with Cardinal Francis George, Japanese Prime Minister Keizo Obuchi, the Duchess of York, tycoon Donald Trump, TV talk show host Jay Leno, or actors Mel Gibson, Tom Hanks, and Bill Cosby. The list goes on and on.

Not all famous visitors have been distinguished. Gangsters Al Capone and Bugs Moran liked to sit near the Cubs' dugout, and bank robber John Dillinger was reported to have spent time in the right-field bleachers, disguised in a postal uniform.

At least one celebrity visitor made himself notorious at Wrigley. In August 2001, former Bears defensive tackle and pro wrestler Steve McMichael took the mike to sing "Take Me Out to the Ball Game" and used the opportunity to blast umpire Angel Hernandez for a close call at home plate. McMichael instantly achieved a tiny place in Wrigley Field history: the first seventh-inning singer to be ejected from the ballpark by an ump.

President Ronald Reagan was no novice on the mound. He portrayed legendary Cubs pitcher Grover Cleveland Alexander in the film *The Winning Team*.

British rock star Elton John's batting grip isn't even appropriate for cricket. It certainly amused David Justice, then with the Atlanta Braves.

Comedian Bill Cosby had some fun with the grounds crew during a visit to the ballpark.

146

TV actor Tom Selleck went further than most celebrities at Wrigley: he took batting practice.

Bill Murray, who grew up in Chicago's north suburbs, took a bizarre turn behind the play-by-play microphone.

"Is that terrible Foley up again? Hey, Foley! Strike out, Foley! I hate everything you stand for!"

—COMEDIAN BILL MURRAY,
AS GUEST BROADCASTER
ON WGN–TV

For every home run, there are countless other runs—

to get more hot dog buns, to roll out the batting cages,

to oversee the turnstiles.

4 HOW IT WORKS

THE CREW

The staff that runs Wrigley Field includes teenagers in the souvenir shop and elderly ushers in the grandstands. The ballpark provides a great job to about one thousand people, but it's not just a job. For most, the Cubs are a passion as well as a profession.

The park wakes up early. For a 1:20 P.M. game, head groundskeeper Roger Baird arrives as early as 6 A.M. "My very first thing I do is put up my Billy and Ernie flags first thing in the morning on the foul poles"—tributes to Hall of Famers Williams and Banks.

Then Baird and his crew get to work on the field, cutting the Kentucky bluegrass every game day. For the infield and sidelines, they use a 27-inch mower like the ones used on golf course greens, custom-made at a cost of $7,000. The outfield is trimmed with a riding mower.

Although Major League Baseball sends out inspectors to check such things as the base paths, mound height, and mound distance, there is no league-regulated grass height because different types of grasses are used in different parts of the country.

Wrigley's grass is considered among the tallest. "I don't think we have the tallest grass—I think we have the *thickest* grass in baseball," Baird said. "Right now we're down to about an inch and a half, and that's as low as you can possibly go with bluegrass."

The crew puts at least 500 gallons of water on the field every day during the season. "We water probably three or four times before the Cubs even come out," Baird said.

"Our dirt is worked over umpteen times on mornings of a game. We hand-spike it every single day, with a nail-dragger." The ground along the wall behind home plate and along the warning track isn't dirt—it's crushed brick.

After working on the grass and dirt, the grounds crew sets up the screens for batting practice, with the batting cage wheeled out of the right-field storage area.

"We're nonstop up till about 10:30. That's when the Cubs come out on a 1:20 game. Me and my assistant [Mike Conoboy] will stay out here during batting practice to keep an eye out to see if there's anything we have to work on.

"Players will ask—they want a little more water, or they want the area worked up a little bit. You get to know the players as the season progresses, and start to learn how they like their position. . . . Pitchers are the same way. Some people like their mound a little wetter, a little drier, a little harder, a little softer. We keep a close eye on who's pitching."

"How many people wouldn't want to work at Wrigley Field?"

—ROGER BAIRD, HEAD GROUNDSKEEPER

152

In the '40s, grounds crew member Harry Hazlewood once asked Cubs pitcher Hi Bithorn, "What do you want me to do with the mound today, Hi?" And Bithorn answered, "Well, you might move it 10 feet closer to home plate."

Groundskeepers can't work miracles. But they can handle a thousand details year-round.

"In the winter, I keep a very close eye on [the field]," Baird said. "Ice is very bad for your grass. That'll smother your grass. You can have real bad problems with snow mold. In fact, this year we did have a slight problem with snow mold. I was actually treating my grass in the middle of February. It was 30-some degrees out here and I was out here putting on a fungicide, which I think helped save me. It's a very nerve-racking job."

By the time the Cubs come out for batting practice at around 10:30 A.M., the park is stirring. Forklifts tear through the concourse, delivering kegs of beer, trash containers, hot dog buns.

The ushers are having their daily meeting, run by security manager Mike Hill, in the grandstand.

Here's why the bases look so white: grounds crew member Brian Helmus paints them before every game.

On a typical day, Hill starts out his briefing with, "What a beautiful day for baseball!" and then gets down to business, past and present.

"I understand the woman who had the heart attack in [section] 123 is fine," he says. "She wanted to check herself out of the hospital this morning."

Today is Old Style tankard day, he tells them. Ushers will be handing out plastic beer tankards to the first 10,000 adults. Some of the tankards will be reserved for the bleachers, he says, but to avoid dangerous flying objects, bleacher fans will get their tankards only on the way out.

A job perk for members of the crew: they can take a nap on top of the dugout.

Wrigley Field was the first major league park to have uniformed, unionized ushers. For about 60 years beginning in 1925, the Cubs relied on a separate company, Andy Frain, to handle ushering. Today, most aspects of "crowd management" are handled internally, and the staff is a combination of young people and retirees.

The oldest usher, Henry Widegren, patrolled the right-field group section until retiring in 2001 at the age of 93—older than Wrigley Field. As a child, Widegren lived within a baseball's throw of the ballpark—across Clark Street, behind where the McDonald's is now—and sometimes he would climb up a pipe to sneak into the park.

In modern times, Widegren only had to climb stairs to get to his ballpark perch. Most fans posed no problem, he said: "People seem to enjoy it. It's really more than a ball game." But occasionally, when people used loud, foul language, he interceded: "I'd tap 'em on the shoulder and tell 'em, 'Be careful now—there's women and children here. It might be your mother or your kids.'"

Also concerned with language is Les Brettman, up in the press box, who handles the electronic messages along the bottom of the scoreboard. Brettman, like Widegren, has had a lifelong love affair with Wrigley Field. Brettman, who is in his seventies, recalls visiting the park for the first time when he was eight years old: "We took the Belmont Avenue streetcar, then we walked down the railroad track that used to be there, and when this thing came into view, it was just like heaven—oh, my God, look at it!"

Much of the baseball trivia that Brettman posts on the message board is provided by Gary Pressy, the Cubs' organist, who works alongside him. Like many Wrigley employees, Pressy is a fan, too.

When it rains, Pressy plays "Pennies from Heaven." When there's a snow-out, as there was in April 2001, Pressy plays Christmas carols.

But his most important tune is "Take Me Out to the Ball Game" during the seventh-inning stretch. He plays it in the key of C usually, though different singers want it done differently. Harry Caray liked it in the key of D. Ann-Margret wanted it in A-flat.

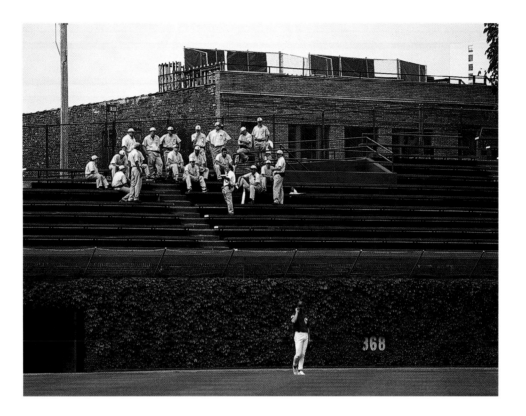

Pressy performed for broadcaster Jack Brickhouse's funeral at Chicago's Holy Name Cathedral, playing a pipe organ for the first time. His tunes: "The Impossible Dream" and the Cubs' anthem "Hey, Hey, Holy Mackerel."

Pressy and Brettman share their press-box booth with Wayne Messmer and Paul Friedman, who work a staggered schedule as public-address announcers. Messmer has a beautiful singing voice and often performs the National Anthem. Paul Friedman also has a golden throat and admits, "One thing I've learned is that if you make a mistake, but if you say it with a deep enough voice, you can get away with it."

Henry Widegren, an usher in his mid-nineties, lived in Wrigleyville before there was a
Wrigley Field.

Messmer and Friedman are following in the footsteps of one of the most
beloved Wrigley Field figures, Pat Pieper, who is remembered for his pregame dec-
laration: "Attention . . . attention please . . . have your pencils . . . and scorecards
ready . . . for the correct lineups . . . for today's ball game."

In 1904, Pieper got a job selling peanuts and popcorn at the West Side Grounds,
and when the Cubs moved to Wrigley in 1916, Pieper snagged the announcer's job.
He would stay at field level and shout through a 14-pound megaphone. During the
game, he sat in a folding chair next to the backstop screen, holding the baseballs
for the umpires and announcing any lineup changes. In 1932, a loudspeaker system

was installed and Pieper retired the megaphone, but he stayed on the field until the 1960s, when he moved up to the press box. Pieper, who died in 1974 at age 88, claimed to have missed only 18 Cubs home games—and none since 1924.

When the gates open at Wrigley Field, the crew gets to work in earnest. Down at the souvenir shop at the main Clark and Addison entrance, business is often so brisk that they've instituted crowd-control measures. A worker stands at the entrance, placing a chain across the door and allowing new people in only when other customers have left.

The scouts, with their radar guns, take their seats behind home plate. Even the visitors love Wrigley Field. "This is by far the most beautiful park," said Phil

162

Message board operator Les Brettman has a commanding view from the press box.

Brettman's partner in the booth, Gary Pressy, plays tunes on the organ and supplies trivia for the message board.

Rizzo, a native of Chicago's Northwest Side who scouts for the Arizona Dia-mondbacks. "It even beats the new parks for scouting because you're so close to the action."

Before the action starts, the umpires take the lineup cards, and as they do, Jimmy Farrell, the umpires' room attendant, quietly goes out to the mound and puts down a clean, new baseball. The game is ready to begin.

Former Cub and current Dodgers broadcaster Rick Monday loves the way the ballpark springs to life: "The thing to do at Wrigley Field is arrive early in the morning, when Wrigley is asleep. This ballpark is asleep, and all of a sudden you begin to see the stadium; first of all, its eyes start to flutter, then people start to

Pat Pieper used his megaphone, and later a microphone, to instruct fans to pick up their pencils and copy down the lineup as he announced it. "He was like a schoolteacher," said Ernie Banks.

164

come in. You arrive here two, three hours before the game, there are people who begin to line up to get into the bleachers. Now the stadium starts to breathe. And then eventually you see the stadium wake up, stand up and stretch its arms, and then the game is played. . . . I think the ballpark actually has a pulse."

And if that's true, if the ballpark indeed has a pulse, the Wrigley Field crew is the life force that drives it.

Oh, say, does Wayne Messmer sing a great National Anthem? Yes, indeed, he does.

166

Jimmy Farrell, umpires' room attendant, places a clean, new baseball on the mound, and it's time to play ball.

The Concessions

In the '40s, you could buy an egg sandwich for 20 cents and a "big wedge of pie" for 15 cents. In 2001, you could get a taco puff for $3 and a frozen banana for $2.

Which is not to suggest that Cubs fans' tastes have changed, only that there are different items on the fringes of the menu.

"This is a back-to-the-basics ballpark, it's an old-time ballpark, it's a traditional ballpark," said concessions boss Curt Radle, "which means it's the hot dogs, the peanuts, the Cracker Jack, the soda, the beer. That's what people come to Wrigley Field for."

"I've seen customers grow up. I've watched some of the fans get married, get divorced, have kids. I'm serving a second generation of fans now."

—DAVE KLEMP, A WRIGLEY VENDOR SINCE 1969

The pace is hectic. "It's a madhouse here," said Radle, "an absolute madhouse." But because of Sammy Sosa, workers at the concession stands can count on at least three breaks during the game. "Lines diminish when Sammy's coming to bat," Radle said.

Most of his staff of 600 manages to enjoy the game while doing their jobs.

"The majority of the people who work here are Cubs fans," said Radle, "and if they're not a Cubs fan, they become a Cubs fan very quickly, because it's an aura in the air here."

Radle himself is too busy to get caught up in auras. "I've been here for seven years; I've never watched a baseball game here," he said.

For vendors who are fans, such as veteran Dave Klemp, it's not always easy to follow the action on the field. "Basically, you turn around after the ball sails over the fence."

In the days when Wrigley Field was still Weeghman Park, fans used to complain about vendors blocking their views, and that's what prompted one of Charles Weeghman's major innovations: the first permanent concession stand in all of baseball. Ironically, Wrigley Field now has more vendors in the stands than most ballparks because there isn't room in the concourse for large concession stands.

Vendors, who are paid on commission plus tips, don't have designated areas. They follow unofficial rules of engagement, such as not going in an aisle where a competitor already is working. But "I encourage the vendors to go everywhere," Radle said.

Beer is the most profitable item for vendors to sell, and under a seniority system, the most experienced vendors sell the suds. Arnie Lipski, a vendor since 1968, recalled that when he started out, he got the less desirable items, including Fresca, a lemon-lime soft drink that Mrs. Wrigley reportedly favored. "If it was 40 degrees, I got Fresca. If it was 90 degrees, I got Cracker Jack."

Today, draft beer is sold at the concession stands, and it's poured from cans by the roving vendors. That's far better than in the late '70s and early '80s, when vendors sold beer prepoured into paper cups. "On a hot day, it actually got warm," Lipski said. "The longer you walked around with it, the worse it would get. The foam would start evaporating, and it would start going flat."

Klemp says vendors keep statistics and standings on who's selling the most, as if they're in a pennant race for beer sales. "There's a lot of competition among vendors. It's not only a job but a lucrative hobby. It's a sport for us."

Being a vendor might be more physically rigorous than being a player. In 1938, it was estimated that the average Wrigley vendor logged 20 miles during a doubleheader. Like any other physical activity, it can be hard on the body. "The common injuries are a shin injury—you bump your leg into a folding chair or metal bar or something—knees, bone spurs," said Klemp. "Sometimes vendors complain about the back. It's like anyone playing sports. Everyone has nagging injuries."

But he's not complaining. "Some people pay $2,000 to join a health club. I get my exercise on the job and get to see the game for free."

No longer does Wrigley Field have portable wagons cooking and selling smokie link sandwiches in the grandstands, which was a feature of the ballpark for

"Start a rally with a popcorn!" "Lemo, lemo, lemonade!"

—POPULAR VENDOR CALLS AT
WRIGLEY FIELD IN THE 1940S

decades. Retired Cubs executive E. R. "Salty" Saltwell recalled the one serious fire at Wrigley, when a smokie link wagon in the right-field corner went ablaze in the '60s.

"In addition to the ball game, the fans got a chance to see the fire department in action," he said.

Hot dogs were called "red hots" in Wrigley Field's early years, and they sold for 10 cents in 1933. Adjusted for inflation, that price would be about $1.40 today, whereas hot dogs in 2002 actually cost $2.25. (The price creep on hot dogs is paltry compared with the quantum leap in the Cubs' greatest operating cost, player salaries. Hack Wilson earned $35,000 in 1931, which would translate to $417,000 in 2002 dollars. In comparison, current Cubs megaslugger Sammy Sosa has a four-

172

year contract that pays him an average of $18 million a year, which is 43 times what Hack earned. Concession prices, in comparison, are peanuts.)

Radle's company, Aramark, which has a contract with the Cubs to provide concessions, also handles souvenir sales inside the park—an idea that came surprisingly late to Wrigley Field. It wasn't until 1947 that the Cubs started selling souvenir baseball caps to the fans.

These days, visors, stuffed animals, and bobbing-head dolls are popular.

The main souvenir store at the Clark and Addison entrance demonstrates many qualities of the ballpark in general. It's undersized, and it's popular. The shop didn't open until the early '80s, and Aramark officials believe it's the major leagues' top-grossing store by square footage. Among the items: a $250 Cubs leather jacket and a $20 Cubs Barbie.

No doubt, Wrigley Field is an easy sale.

The Tickets

Individual-game Cubs tickets usually go on sale on the third Friday in February, and it's a mad scramble for the best seats. Even in the worst winter weather, crowds of bundled-up ticket buyers gather outside Wrigley Field. Of course, fans who don't want to ski to the ticket booth can surf instead—at cubs.com. Either way, the flurry of sales is intense.

"It's wild," said Frank Maloney, director of ticket operations, "because the initial demand here is about as heavy as it is anywhere in baseball. And generally, in that first Friday-Saturday-Sunday period, we sell about 300,000 tickets. It stresses our computer system."

Maloney, former assistant football coach at the University of Michigan and former head football coach at Syracuse University, knows how to pick up the blitz.

174

"The highest demand day is Saturdays," Maloney said. "Used to be followed up by Sunday. I'd say it's now very close between Friday and Sunday for the number two spot. As far as teams, Cardinals way out in front."

Next biggest in demand: games against the White Sox and the Milwaukee Brewers.

The Cubs take special orders, when possible.

"We get requests for exact, specific seats," Maloney said. "People will send us one of their old stubs, or a Xeroxed copy, and say, 'I'd like this seat.' And if it's there, we sell it to them."

Also, "A person wanted to buy two seats just for himself because he was extra large, and wanted us to take out the thing in the middle that separates the seats. We did it as a season ticket."

World Series tickets are printed in early September for all teams still in contention. Unfortunately, the Cubs' Series tickets haven't been needed since 1945.

175

Maloney makes no accommodation for the scalpers, though. Under Illinois law, "ticket brokers" can legally resell tickets at a higher price, with the markup described as a service charge, as long as they stay off-site.

It may be legal, but that doesn't mean the Cubs like it.

"It's like the black market in World War II," said Maloney. "It depletes the market. They drain the supply. They force the poor guy from Keokuk, Iowa, to come here and he can't get tickets and I think foolishly goes over there [to ticket brokers] and pays an exorbitant amount."

For a regular-season game, Maloney has heard of $25 or $30 tickets going for $300. "I've heard 'em as high as $1,500 for a playoff," he said.

There's also the problem of people hawking tickets right outside the park, which is illegal. Fans should beware of people selling such tickets—if you think you're buying four bleacher seats, you might find that the top ticket is a bleacher ticket but the other three are upper-deck tickets for a game that took place last week. And remember: SRO means "standing room only," not "second row only," no matter what a ticket hawker says.

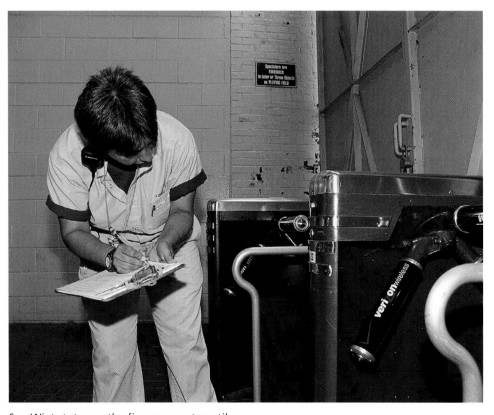

Sue Wiatr totes up the figures on a turnstile.

HIDDEN WRIGLEY

Wrigley has its catacombs, a succession of rooms and passageways and caverns under the stands where the players and their supporting cast wait in the wings for the big show.

There are the home and visitors' locker rooms, the umpires' dressing room, a weight room, a trainer's room, a video room, and even something they call "the rain room," where the Cubs get a weather satellite feed and have phone access to the National Weather Service.

Sosa plays soccer in the locker room.

Head groundskeeper Roger Baird is a big believer in the rain room. "I try and get the best idea when rain is coming and try and pinpoint how hard, how long it's going to last, and I try to keep the umpires and our team well advised of what's going to happen. If I know it's coming, a real good chance that it's going to hit us, I've got to have all my men ready, because the quicker you can have that canvas down, the less damage you're going to have to the field."

No system is perfect, of course. On August 23, 1999, the Cubs delayed a game for nearly two hours because rain appeared imminent. The only problem was, nothing fell from the sky. "Everybody's telling you it should be pouring over you," said Baird, "and it's not pouring."

Finally, the deluge arrived, and the game was rained out—after a rainless delay of nearly two hours, which would've been enough time to get in an official game.

When the weather is lousy, the Cubs skip batting practice outdoors and instead use a batting cage under the right-field bleachers.

Another part of Wrigley that's hidden—unless you have a ticket—is the mezzanine suite area. Wrigley's skyboxes aren't much different from those anywhere else, but they do serve a special purpose for the rest of the ballpark. There are no replays on the scoreboard, of course, so if there's a close call, fans can wait for the reaction of the people in the skyboxes, where there are televisions. If a chorus of groans emanates from there, the whole ballpark knows that the ump blew the call.

One section of Wrigley's history is hidden in plain sight. That's the nondescript building next to the Waveland entrance to the left-field grandstand. The building,

The "rain room" helps the Cubs keep track of the weather.

now used by Aramark, the concession company, used to be the six-room apartment where head groundskeeper Bobby Dorr lived with his family. The house was
built in 1923 on the orders of William Wrigley, and one nickname for the ballpark
in the old days was "Bobby Dorr's House." After groundskeepers stopped using
the house, it was converted to Cubs office space. Cubs carpenter Fred Jacobs
recalled doing renovation work there in 1989. "They were looking for more
space," Jacobs said. "There was this wall in there. I thought, 'What the heck is that
there for?' I opened up the wall and found this bathtub in there."

The video room, where players can analyze their pitches and swings, was equipped at a cost
of $750,000 in the 1990s.

Kerry Wood works out on a running machine in the exercise room.

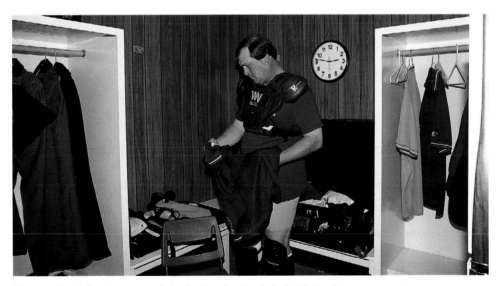

The umpires' dressing room is tucked under the left-field stands.

Clubhouse fixture Yosh Kawano has worked behind the scenes at Wrigley for more than five decades. He got his start as a Cubs batboy in 1935, and after serving as a military policeman in World War II, he returned to Wrigley Field to work in both the home and visitor clubhouses.

Home clubhouse manager Tom Hellman sews a new number on a uniform.

Chris Maudlin cleans spikes.

Some of the Cubs hold a Sunday chapel in the weight room, led by baseball chaplain Noel Castellanos (right).

Sosa gets limbered up in the locker room and then crouches in the tunnel leading to the dugout, gathering his intensity before a game.

There's a capacity crowd of memories inside Wrigley Field.

It's a ballpark that takes measure of its history

even as it marches into the future.

5 LEGACY

SPECIAL MOMENTS

Amazing things have occurred at Wrigley Field, occasionally on schedule, often by surprise. Some of these spectacular moments have been recounted already in this book: the 1984 "Sandberg game," for example, and the first night game. Here are others, in chronological order:

May 2, 1917: The Double No-Hitter

It was the greatest pitchers' duel in baseball history. Cincinnati's Fred Toney faced the Cubs' Jim "Hippo" Vaughn. Through nine innings, neither had given up a hit. In the top of the tenth, the Reds' Larry Kopf hit a single to right to break up Vaughn's no-hitter and then advanced to third on an error. With two out, Jim Thorpe, the famed Olympic star, hit a roller down the third-base line. It was fielded by Vaughn, who figured he couldn't get the swift Thorpe at first and therefore threw home to try for Kopf. But Cubs catcher Art Wilson was expecting the throw to go to first, and Vaughn's throw bounced off his chest.

"I'd play for half my salary if I could hit in this dump all the time."

—BABE RUTH

In the bottom of the tenth, Toney closed out his end of the no-hitter. In the clubhouse afterward, Vaughn declared to disbelieving reporters, "It's just another game."

October 1, 1932: Babe Ruth's "Called Shot"

It was Game 3 of the World Series, and Ruth was the least popular player in town. He'd already hit a three-run home run in the first inning, and here he was coming up again in the fifth inning, with the score tied 4–4. Pitcher Guy Bush was insulting him from the Cubs' dugout. One fan threw a lemon at him as he strode to the plate. The crowd was electric and abusive. Pitcher Charlie Root got two strikes on Ruth, and then the Sultan of Swat made some sort of gesture. The legend is that he pointed to center field to indicate where he planned to hit the next pitch. The truth is probably less tidy.

Cubs catcher Gabby Hartnett said Ruth "held up the index finger, looked at our dugout, not the outfield, and said, 'It only takes one to hit.'"

Root insisted: "He didn't point. If he had, I'd have knocked him on his fanny." According to the Cubs' pitcher: "Babe did lift a finger toward our dugout after the first strike and two after the second. The count was two and two when I threw him a curve on the outside and he hit it over my head and into the bleachers. But he didn't point."

Cubs public-address announcer Pat Pieper, who was stationed by the backstop, said, "I was sitting within a few feet of Ruth when he pointed and it wasn't any myth. He was pointing toward the bleachers. You can forget that 'indicating the count' stuff. Ruth called his shot, pure and simple."

The only sure fact is that Ruth homered into the center-field bleachers.

A year later, when Ruth was asked whether he'd called his shot, he said, "Hell, no. Only a damned fool would do a thing like that." But later, his autobiography claimed that he had indeed done it.

Who knows what to believe? After the game, seven people outside the gates claimed to be holding Ruth's home-run ball. As *Washington Post* sportswriter Shirley Povich put it, "Who could ever forget the scene, even if he never saw it?"

Babe Ruth's daughter, Julia Ruth Stevens, re-creates his "Called Shot" during a 2001 visit to the ballpark.

September 28, 1938: The Homer in the Gloamin'

The Pittsburgh Pirates led the Cubs by seven games going into September, but the Pirates were ahead by only a half game when the two teams met at Wrigley Field with four games left on the schedule. It was a 5–5 tie going into the ninth, and the umpires had decided that there'd be no extra innings because of the impending darkness, the gloaming. After the Cubs held the Pirates scoreless in the top of the ninth, Pittsburgh hurler Mace Brown got two outs. Then Gabby Hartnett, the Cubs' player-manager, came to bat and got hold of one. "A lot of people have told me they didn't know the ball was in the bleachers. Well, I did. Maybe I was the only one in the park who did. I knew it the moment I hit it," said Hartnett, who was mobbed in the biggest home-plate celebration ever at Wrigley Field. The clout gave the Cubs irresistible momentum—for the National League pennant, that is. After that, they lost to the Yankees in four straight World Series games.

June 30, 1959: Two Balls in Play

OK, folks, time to concentrate. Bob Anderson is pitching for the Cubs, with Stan "the Man" Musial at bat for the St. Louis Cardinals. A pitch goes past everybody. Catcher Sammy Taylor thinks it's a foul tip and doesn't go after it. Musial thinks

Pandemonium erupts as Gabby Hartnett trots home after "the Homer in the Gloamin'."

it's ball four and heads to first. Cubs third baseman Alvin Dark thinks it might be a wild pitch and starts running after it. The ballboy thinks it's a foul and grabs it, tossing it to public-address announcer Pat Pieper. Who knows what home-plate umpire Vic Delmore is thinking: he pulls out another ball and hands it to Taylor, who gives it to Anderson. Meanwhile, Dark gets the original ball from Pieper just as Musial rounds first and breaks for second. Shortstop Ernie Banks is covering second, and both Dark and Anderson throw their baseballs to him. Banks catches the throw from Dark and tags Musial. But Musial, seeing Anderson's throw go into center field, ignores Banks's tag and heads for third. Centerfielder Bobby Thomson gathers Anderson's ball and fires it past third base, into the Cubs' dugout. The umpires seem as confused as everyone else. Delmore rules Musial out at second while ump Al Barlick says he's safe at first. Eventually, Musial is called out, and the Cardinals play the game under protest (which they drop after winning 4–1). The real loser is Delmore, who is dumped from his job at season's end.

By the way, if you're scoring, the play went ballboy-announcer-5-6 with ball number one, and umpire-2-1-8-dugout with ball number two.

195

December 29, 1963: Bears Win NFL Title

Days before the game, the Bears covered the field with hay and put a tarpaulin over it, and then they placed aircraft-hangar heaters around the field to blow air under the tarp. But nothing could combat the frigid onslaught of a Chicago winter. When they removed the tarp and got ready to play the NFL championship game against the New York Giants, the field quickly froze solid. The footing was so unpredictable that the Bears' trainers laid out six kinds of shoes for the players.

By halftime, the temperature was seven degrees. It was the kind of day when the lucky people were those who couldn't get tickets. Still, 45,802 hardy souls attended the game, including New York Mayor Robert Wagner and Chicago Mayor Richard J. Daley. The game was broadcast on big screens via closed-circuit television to a variety of locations, including Chicago's McCormick Place, which collected $21,128.52 in admissions.

The game wasn't decided until the last minute, when Bears defensive back Richie Petibon intercepted Y. A. Tittle's pass in the end zone.

Halas, at age 68, declared after the game: "I guess today's game proves that if you live long enough, everything nice you want to happen will happen."

May 12, 1970: Ernie Banks's 500th Home Run

For the man who played 2,528 games as a Cub without ever reaching postseason play—and without ever complaining about it—the grandstands should have been packed. But it was a rainy, miserable day, and even though it was a special senior citizens discount day, only 5,264 fans were there to witness Ernie Banks's 500th home run. It came in the second inning against Atlanta Braves pitcher Pat Jarvis. Later, Jarvis said the letter-high fastball was "right where I wanted it," and it was right where Banks wanted it, too. His hit sailed over leftfielder Rico Carty's head, smacked into the bleachers, and bounced back onto the field, where Carty retrieved it and gave it to Ferguson Jenkins in the bullpen for safekeeping.

Banks, who was 39 at the time, declared, "It was senior citizens day—a great day."

September 2, 1972: Milt Pappas's Near-Perfect Game

It had been a tough season for Milt Pappas. He'd already had 30 cortisone shots to take the sting out of his elbow trouble. Now he had a bad cold, and he wanted to call in sick. But his wife, Carole, talked him out of it, persuading him to show up and pitch against the San Diego Padres.

And so he did. Twenty-six batters later, Pappas was looking at a perfect game, if only he could retire pinch hitter Larry Stahl. He got a one-two count, then threw three straight pitches that were called balls by umpire Bruce Froemming. The last two were fairly close, but outside, according to newspaper accounts. They may have been low, too. Froemming said after the game: "They were what we call shoe-shiners, well below the knee." Ron Santo, watching from third base, thought

Bleacher fans await another blast by Ernie Banks.

Pappas's fourth ball looked "like a knee-high strike." Pappas said, "I was hoping he would sympathize with me and give me a call. But they were balls, no question about it."

Pappas got the next batter out, settling for a no-hitter—the last one thrown by a Cub in the 20th century.

Number 4,191: Pete Rose's record-tying hit

200

September 8, 1985: Pete Rose Ties All-Time Hits Record

It wouldn't have happened if Steve Trout hadn't fallen off of his bicycle. Trout, the Cubs' left-handed pitcher, had a bike accident and hurt his hand, and he had to skip his start. In his place came right-handed pitcher Reggie Patterson, which meant that Reds player-manager Pete Rose, a switch hitter who batted better against righties, was starting.

Back in Cincinnati, Reds owner Marge Schott was not pleased. Rose was only two hits away from tying Ty Cobb's all-time hits record, and Schott wanted him to make history before a crowd full of Reds fans, including her pet dog Schottzie, not in front of strangers at Wrigley Field.

In his first at-bat, Rose got hit number 4,190, a single to left. He grounded out the second time, then came up in the fifth inning and smacked number 4,191, a single to right off Patterson to tie the record. When Rose reached base, Cubs first baseman Leon Durham told him, "Just stand still. I want to get some TV time."

For the rest of the game, Rose's teammates, including Dave Parker, urged him to take himself out of the game, to avoid breaking the record on the road. "Parker kept coming up to me and saying, 'Don't do it, don't do it.' I told him I've got to bat. We've got to try to win," Rose recalled.

His fourth at-bat was a sharp ground-out to short. Then in the ninth inning, after a two-hour, four-minute rain delay, with the skies darkening shortly before 6 P.M., Rose struck out swinging against reliever Lee Smith. He would indeed break the record at home, whether he liked it or not. As for the tying of the record, Rose confessed some confusion: "Here I am, trying to please everybody and I got 30,000 yelling for me here and one lady back in Cincinnati who, every time I get a hit, she's kicking the dog."

"Wrigley keeps making history."

—PETE ROSE

201

May 6, 1998: Kerry Wood Strikes Out 20

Kerry Wood came into the game as a 20-year-old rookie with a 2–2 record and a 5.89 earned run average. Nine innings later, he had earned his own tribute flag on the roof of Wrigley Field's upper deck.

Facing the hard-hitting Houston Astros, Wood struck out the side four times and allowed only two balls to reach the outfield. His only flaws were a hit batsman in the sixth and a scrub single in the third by Ricky Gutierrez, a future teammate.

The last out of the game, a strikeout of Derek Bell, tied the major league strikeout record set by Roger Clemens when he was with the Boston Red Sox.

"It was just one of those days when everything you throw is across the plate," Wood said. "It just felt like I was playing catch."

"It sounds like a ridiculous thing to say, but Kerry's game had to be the greatest game anybody's ever pitched at Wrigley Field."

—FORMER CUBS MANAGER
JIM RIGGLEMAN

202

Kerry Wood fires away at the Houston Astros during his record-tying performance.

Fans tally Wood's Ks during his 20-strikeout game. The sign reading E-5 indicates one fan's opinion that the only hit given up by Wood should've been scored as an error. The hit, a single, skipped past the glove of third baseman Kevin Orie, who reached for the ball but did not dive.

203

September 13, 1998: Sammy Sosa's 61st and 62nd Home Runs

Sosa's career with the Cubs has been one long highlight film, which makes it difficult to pick out just one game, or one exploit, that illustrates his accomplishments. After all, he's hit 60 home runs in three different seasons—the only major league player to do that.

A fond memory for many fans is the 1998 home-run race between Sosa and St. Louis's Mark McGwire. On September 8, McGwire hit number 62 to break Roger Maris's single-season home-run record. McGwire's record-breaker came against the Cubs at Busch Stadium in St. Louis, and Sosa graciously hugged his rival in celebration.

Five days later, with the Cubs facing the Milwaukee Brewers, it was Beanie Baby Day at Wrigley Field. The first 10,000 kids got a beanbag toy named Gracie the Swan, in honor of first baseman Mark Grace. The crowd was standing room only, 40,846.

Sosa was trailing McGwire 62–60 in the home-run race. In the fifth inning, Sosa hit a two-run homer onto Waveland Avenue off Bronswell Patrick.

In the ninth, Sosa took a fastball from Eric Plunk and sent another missile onto Waveland Avenue, tying him with McGwire. The public-address system played "Thus Spake Zarathustra" as Sosa circled the bases and took three curtain calls.

When the game went into extra innings, fans thought Sosa might have a chance to pass McGwire in the home-run race. It was almost a disappointment when Grace came to bat, with Sosa on deck, and hit a game-winning home run for an 11–10 Cubs victory.

But Sosa was happy with his day's work.

"Unbelievable," he said. "It was something that I can't even believe I was doing."

He and McGwire were tied with 62. "I told Mark to wait and I guess he listened to me," said Sosa. "We will just have to see how it goes."

In the end, it went McGwire's way, 70 to 66. But Sosa received the National League's Most Valuable Player Award, leading the Cubs into the playoffs.

September 27, 2001: Wrigley Wrapped in the Flag

The terrorist attacks of September 11 stunned the nation and led to a one-week postponement of the season. The Cubs' first home game afterward was an emotional display, with American flags replacing the tribute flags along the upper-deck roofline and giant flags unfurled from the rooftops as Wayne Messmer sang "The Star-Spangled Banner." Students from nearby LeMoyne Elementary School led the crowd in the Pledge of Allegiance. Firefighters, police officers, and members of the American Red Cross lined up along the baselines as honored guests, and Cubs catcher Joe Girardi declared: "We have learned the true meaning of the word *hero*. . . . We salute you." Sammy Sosa was up to the occasion, hitting a home run, then taking a small American flag from coach Billy Williams as he rounded first base and waving it as he trotted around the bases.

Cubs line up for America, including (in front row) Ricky Gutierrez, Todd Van Poppel, Kerry Wood, Eric Young, and Sammy Sosa.

TRIBUTES

Monuments have been built into Wrigley Field to honor the people who helped build the park's popularity.

Even before fans go through the turnstiles, they may encounter the Harry Caray statue on Addison near the Friendly Confines Café. The work of art was created by Omri Amrany, an Israeli native whose Chicago studio also produced the Michael Jordan statue outside United Center. The cosculptor, Lou Cella, a life-long Cubs fan, used to be a peanut vendor at Wrigley.

When the statue was unveiled in 1999, Harry's partner, Steve Stone, said, "I couldn't think of a better place for him to be in perpetuity than in the midst of the bars here."

Harry's grandson, Chip, quipped, "I know what he'd be saying: 'Hey, I'm a lot better looking than that!'"

At first, practical jokers would put a beer can in the statue's outstretched hand. But, in general, that trend has evaporated. After the September 11 attacks, an American flag was found in Harry's hand.

Another broadcasting legend, Jack Brickhouse, was honored in 1999 with the "Hey Hey" signs on the foul poles. (A statue of Brickhouse sits outside the WGN Radio studios at the Tribune Tower downtown.)

The flags along the rim of the upper-deck roof commemorate the ballpark's greatest seasons and memorable characters. On the left-field side, the years of the Cubs' World Series, league, and division titles are marked. On the right-field side, the flags pay tribute to noted people and events in Wrigley history:

42/JR—Jackie Robinson's number

8/HAWK—Andre Dawson's number and nickname

PKW on both sides—Philip Knight Wrigley

191/HACK—Hack Wilson's major league record RBI total for the 1930 season

31/FJ—Ferguson Jenkins's number

66/SAMMY—Sammy Sosa's home-run total in 1998

10/SANTO—Ron Santo's number

23/RYNO—Ryne Sandberg's number

20/KW—Kerry Wood's major league tying strikeout total on May 6, 1998

17/GRACE—Mark Grace's number

ARNE/WGN—Honoring the man who made Cubs broadcasts great, producer-director Arne Harris, who died in 2001

A new feature was added to the ballpark in 2002 to honor the Chicago Cubs' Walk of Fame inductees. Along the concourse are colorful banners in tribute to broadcasters Lou Boudreau, Jack Brickhouse, and Harry Caray; public-address announcer Pat Pieper; clubhouse assistant Yosh Kawano; and players Cap Anson, Ernie Banks, Glenn Beckert, Bill Buckner, Phil Cavarretta, Andre Dawson, Stan Hack, Gabby Hartnett, Rogers Hornsby, Ferguson Jenkins, Don Kessinger, Andy

208

Pafko, Rick Reuschel, Ryne Sandberg, Ron Santo, Hank Sauer, Rick Sutcliffe, Billy Williams, and Hack Wilson.

Banks and Williams also have their names and numbers on flags atop the foul poles.

Williams, now in the Cubs' front office after a stint as first-base coach, can gaze up and bask in the tribute every home game.

"You get a good feeling when you look at that," he said. "You look at that and you think 'job well done.' . . . You think it'll be there for a while, because they're not going to tear down Wrigley Field. My children's children can come out to Wrigley Field . . . and I know that when they come out here, they will be proud to sit by somebody and say, 'You know that number up there, that was my grand-father's number.' You leave a legacy, and that's what makes you proud."

THE FUTURE

It's safe to say that someday baseball will outgrow the old ballpark at Clark and Addison. Unless Wrigley outlives baseball, which is another scary notion.

Rest assured, neither Wrigley Field nor baseball is going away anytime soon. Tribune Company has made a commitment to the ballpark, taking aggressive steps to inspect and improve the facility, from girders to guardrails to grandstands.

"If they keep putting money and maintenance into it, it could last indefinitely," said Fred Jacobs, Wrigley Field's carpenter. "There are buildings in Europe that are 800 or 1,000 years old."

That's true, of course. The Colosseum in Rome is still standing. But then again, the Lions aren't playing there anymore.

A park as old as Wrigley depends on the goodwill of its owners, the tolerance of its neighbors, and the loyalty of its fans.

Tribune Company has worked hard to be a positive force in the neighborhood. Its Cubs Care program gives grants to nearby playlots and park field houses, and it funds local senior programs, food pantries, and family shelters. Wrigley Field is still

Cubs president and chief executive officer Andy MacPhail watches batting practice with Ron Santo and Billy Williams.

considered an asset to the Lake View neighborhood. If there weren't advantages in living around the ballpark, the real-estate agents wouldn't call the area Wrigleyville.

And the fans? They keep coming, in droves. They come from London and Little Rock, from Tokyo and Tinley Park.

The masses want Wrigley Field to stay. But there are myths surrounding Wrigley that diminish its value as a baseball field, that turn it into a mirage instead of a ballpark.

One is the idea that the Cubs enjoy being "lovable losers" and don't care whether they field a winning team as long as people keep coming to the ballpark.

It's true that the park has gained a celebrity status independent of the Cubs. Wrigley isn't just a venue; it's a destination. And it's also true that, in 1948, the Cubs became the first team to draw a million fans with a last-place team. The Cubs have sometimes drawn well with bad teams, but it's not something to be relied on. The down days of the early '60s speak to the danger of that, and the dizzying success of 1984 testifies to the value of a winning team.

Tribune Company, which is generally a media corporation, has been accused of caring more about TV ratings than the successful turning of the double play. "The Cubs are a pimple on the Tribune Company's financial statement. They're not a core business," said Pat Gillick, an executive with the Seattle Mariners.

But the Cubs have their own set of ratings—the National League Central Division standings—and there's no question that a winning team is the best guarantee of the future of Wrigley Field. The ballpark was at 91 percent of capacity in 2001; winning is the way to improve attendance at the fringes, in April and September . . . and, fans hope, in October.

"The greatest marketing idea of all time is winning consistently," said John McDonough, the Cubs' vice president for marketing and broadcasting.

Cubs management, like its fans, dreams of a World Series at Wrigley Field.

"It would be mind-boggling. You would need the National Guard, the militia, the state police, the local police," said McDonough. "There would be euphoria. There would probably be a three- to five-month hangover. The [marketing] spin would be a decade. People would come to the park just to say, 'This is where the Cubs won the World Series.'"

Believe it: the Cubs want to win.

Another myth that could shorten the ballpark's future is the idea that Wrigley Field is stuck in time and must be imprisoned in that time capsule. This is preservation at its most misguided. Columnist and Cubs fan George Will, writing in favor of lights, bemoaned the view of Wrigley Field as "a little Williamsburg, a cute artifact of historic preservation." Wrigley can't survive unless it remains a successful baseball park. There are plenty of other places to get a suntan.

"Anyone can have a
bad century."
—JACK BRICKHOUSE

Mark McGuire, Cubs executive vice president for business operations, said, "You could sit here and say we're going to keep this shrine, this museum, and not change a single thing, and frankly I don't know how you could compete, unless you have an owner who's willing to subsidize losses of tens of millions of dollars."

The trick is to make changes—improvements, we all hope—without ruining the old ballpark, without killing the golden goose. But freezing Wrigley Field in time, or turning the clock backward, is not an option. It's not even a good idea.

If we wanted to take Wrigley back in time, we'd repaint the big doors in the outfield a fire-engine red, the way they were in the '70s, instead of the tasteful green they are now. We'd take the outfield distance markers off the brick and put them back on plywood markers attached to the brick, the way they were before 1981. And we'd repaint the scoreboard reddish brown, the way it was until the mid-'40s, when it was given that perfect shade of green that it is today. In fact, if we wanted to take Wrigley back to its original condition, we'd dynamite the scoreboard, apply an herbicide to the ivy, and rip off the upper deck, too.

Truth is, Wrigley is better today than ever—better maintained, more functional, more beautiful, more alive. Someday it'll all be gone, but not today, not this year. And it's up to us to enjoy it now, in its heyday.

As Chip Caray put it, "There's going to come a point in time, I'm sure, God forbid I'm alive when it happens, but there's going to come a point in time where this ballpark—like Tiger Stadium, like old Atlanta Stadium, like Candlestick Park—outlives its usefulness as far as the sport is concerned, and I think the day that that happens is the day when all of us will die a little bit. Because it hurts to see your childhood disappear. And I'm hoping that whenever that day comes, it will be a long, long way from now."

With luck, and with the love of its fans, it will be a very long time from now.

May Wrigley Field outlive us all.

NOTES

PART I: THE FRIENDLY CONFINES

The History

Among the books helpful in tracking the evolution of Wrigley Field are *Green Cathedrals* by Philip J. Lowry, *The Game Is Never Over* by Jim Langford, *The Million-to-One Team* by George Castle, *The Chicago Cubs* by Warren Brown, *A Day at the Park* by William Hartel, *Veeck—As in Wreck* by Bill Veeck with Ed Linn, *So You Think You're a Die-Hard Cubs Fan* by Bob Logan, *Essential Cubs* by Doug Myers, *Cub Fan Mania* by Bob Ibach and Ned Colletti, and *Day by Day in Chicago Cubs History* by Art Ahrens and Eddie Gold, edited by Buck Peden. The ballparks.com website by Paul Munsey and Cory Suppes was also a reliable source. Richard Cahan's article in the February 1996 issue of *Vine Line*, "Lucky Charlie's Edifice of Beauty," offers a solid account of the architectural changes in the park, as well as providing quotes by historian Doug Bukowski and architect Philip Bess that are used in this book. Interesting details on Charles Weeghman's Federal League exploits appear in Richard Lindberg's article in *Chicago History* magazine in Spring 1981, "The Chicago Whales and the Federal League of American Baseball, 1914–15," and also in an article by Vickie Pietryga in a Chicago Cubs publication. Excellent profiles of William Wrigley Jr. and P. K. Wrigley appear in F. Richard Ciccone's *Chicago and the American Century*. Other dependable sources of information about P. K. Wrigley are Castle's book and Jay Robert Nash's *Makers and Breakers of Chicago*. The precise figures on the season-ticket increase from 1984 to '85 come from Cubs ticket director Frank Maloney: a jump from 7,572 to 25,051. (Converting partial season-ticket plans to "full-season equivalents," the increase was from 4,431 to 13,179.)

The Vines

A fine account of the planting of the ivy is in *Veeck—As in Wreck* by Bill Veeck with Ed Linn. Veeck also is quoted in *Cub Fan Mania* by Bob Ibach and Ned Colletti. The Lou Novikoff story comes from Warren Brown's *The Chicago Cubs*, the grandfather of all great Cubs books. Andre Dawson's observations are in *The Chicago Cubs: Memories and Memorabilia of the Wrigley Wonders*, text by Bruce Chadwick, photography by David M. Spindel. Other sources: *Essential Cubs* by Doug Myers and *Ballparks* by Robert von Goeben.

The Bleachers

Several of the stories here were first encountered in Rick Phalen's wonderful oral history, *Our Chicago Cubs*, which includes Palmer Pyle's reminiscence of the Right Field Bleacher Choir and broadcaster Mike Murphy's recollections about the Bleacher Bums, including the story of Lou Brock and the mice. Other key sources: *Day by Day in Chicago Cubs History* by Art Ahrens and Eddie Gold, *Essential Cubs* by Doug Myers, *Cub Fan Mania* by Bob Ibach and Ned Colletti, and *Ballparks of North America* by Michael Benson. The Rick Monday quote is from Carrie Muskat's *Banks to Sandberg to Grace*, a finely produced oral history that is must reading for Cubs fans. The Mudcat Grant quote is from *The Cubbies—Quotations on the Chicago Cubs* by Bob Chieger. By the way, Eric Partridge's *A Dictionary of Slang and Unconventional English* explains that the term *bleachers* comes from the fact that the sun would bleach the clothes of people who sat in the sun-drenched seats.

The Scoreboard

The quote by Jimmy Dudley is from Curt Smith's *Storied Stadiums*. The Moe Drabowsky story about sign stealing is based on the account in Carrie Muskat's *Banks to Sandberg to Grace*.

The Wind

The Ryne Sandberg and Mitch Williams quotes are from Carrie Muskat's *Banks to Sandberg to Grace*. Jim Lefebvre is quoted in *The Chicago Cubs: Memories and Memorabilia of the Wrigley Wonders*, text by Bruce Chadwick, photography by David M. Spindel. Tom Skilling's analysis of the Wrigley winds appeared on the *Chicago Tribune* weather page, with credit to Skilling assistants Steve Kahn and Thomas Valle.

The Lights

The lights issue is well chronicled in *The Million-to-One Team* by George Castle and *Essential Cubs* by Doug Myers, as well as in articles by Dave Nightingale in *The Sporting News* and an essay by Phil Vettel in *Chicago Days*, a book produced by the staff of the *Chicago Tribune*. The Jeff Pentland quote is from the *Chicago Tribune*. The William Shlensky lawsuit is detailed in the *Chicago American* newspaper and in Edgar Munzel's article in *The Sporting News*. Larry Bowa's quote comes from *The Sporting News*. The Representative Dunn quote is from *The Cubbies—Quotations on the Chicago Cubs* by Bob Chieger. *Vine Line* is a great source for details on the first night game.

Part II: A Cast of Thousands

The Players

Two books by Eddie Gold and Art Ahrens, *The Golden Era Cubs* and *The New Era Cubs*, offer hilarious and fascinating profiles of Cubs players, including the Ken Holtzman quotation. The Black Sox story is from John Thorn's *A Century of Baseball Lore*. The Cardenal and Fontenot stories are in *Tales from the Cubs Dugout* by Pete Cava. The Kingman story is cited in George F. Will's very readable collection of essays, *Bunts*. The quotations of Jack Brickhouse and Andre Dawson are from George Castle's *The Million-to-One Team*, which may be the single best book explaining the mystifying management moves by the Cubs during the 20th century. Alvin Dark is quoted in Doug Myers's *Essential Cubs*. The Ernie Banks quote is in *The Chicago Cubs: Memories and Memorabilia of the Wrigley Wonders*, text by Bruce Chadwick, photography by David M. Spindel. Harry Chiti is quoted in *Take Me Out to the Cubs Game* by John C. Skipper.

The Fans

Bob Chieger's *The Cubbies—Quotations on the Chicago Cubs* is a wonderful book to page through and is where we found the Joe Garagiola quote. Bob Sirott's recollection is from his essay in the *Chicago Tribune* in August 2001. The Mark Grace comment is from *The Chicago Cubs: Memories and Memorabilia of the Wrigley Wonders*, text by Bruce Chadwick, photography by David M. Spindel. Carrie Muskat's *Banks to Sandberg to Grace* provides the quote from Mike Krukow. The quotes by Jerry Pritikin and Jack Brickhouse are from *So You Think You're a Die-Hard Cubs Fan* by Bob Logan.

The Neighbors

Ballparks of North America by Michael Benson explains the attitudes in the neighborhood in 1914. *Essential Cubs* by Doug Myers offers the stories about Tom

Browning and Dave Kingman. The history of Murphy's Bleachers is detailed on the bar's website, murphysbleachers.com. The quotes of Sharon Streicher and Keith Hernandez are in *The Cubbies—Quotations on the Chicago Cubs* by Bob Chieger. The details of the Sosa homer come from coverage by Roman Modrowski, Toni Ginnetti, and Eddie Gold of the *Chicago Sun-Times*. Glenallen Hill's gargantuan blast is re-created from reportage by Mike Harrington in the *Buffalo News* and by Mark Brown in an investigative story in the *Chicago Sun-Times*, which did the rare thing in sports journalism: discovering hard fact amid sloppy myth. "Eamus catuli" is deciphered in an article by Tara Deering in the *Chicago Tribune*. The restaurant sign is described in an essay by George F. Will.

The Ballhawks

The quote of Mike Steinbacher and other details come from Elliott Harris and Roman Modrowski of the *Chicago Sun-Times*. Accounts by the Associated Press and Helene Elliott of the *Los Angeles Times* also were helpful sources. The Sammy Sosa quote is from Mario Fox of the Associated Press.

The Broadcasters

Chicago Tribune articles by David Condon and Richard Dozer help explain Bob Elson. Doug Myers's *Essential Cubs, The Game Is Never Over* by Jim Langford, and *So You Think You're a Die-Hard Cubs Fan* by Bob Logan are other invaluable sources on broadcasting at Wrigley. But if you call the Museum of Broadcast Communications in Chicago and ask for an expert on Cubs radio and television, they'll refer you to sportswriter George Castle. His books *The Million-to-One Team* and *I Remember Harry Caray* (written with Rich Wolfe) paint a vivid picture of the broadcasting of the Cubs. Jim Frey's quote is from *I Remember Harry Caray*. The Harry Caray quote about Pavarotti is from *The Cubbies—Quotations on the Chicago Cubs* by Bob Chieger. The Caray–Steve Stone exchange about Mike Marshall is from a Steve Wulf article in *Sports Illustrated*. The Caray quote to Reagan is from the *Washington Post*. The story about Caray hanging up on the president was related to the authors of this book by both Stone and Arne Harris; the exact wording of Caray's quote is taken from *Where's Harry?* by Steve Stone with Barry Rozner.

PART III: SIDESHOWS

The Bears

A key resource for this chapter is Richard Whittingham, whose books *The Bears: A 75-Year Celebration* and *Bears: In Their Own Words* include the quotes by Gale Sayers, Dick Butkus, and George Halas (the Bronko Nagurski story). George Vass's *George Halas and the Chicago Bears* offers interesting details, including the Tex

Schramm quote. The Jack Brickhouse quote comes from Ed McGregor's article in *Vine Line* in December 1993. Other helpful sources: the Chicago Bears media guide and *Halas on Halas* by George Halas with Gwen Morgan and Arthur Veysey. The calculation of NFL games at Wrigley and other venues is based on information provided by various NFL teams, including the Bears, along with data from Joe Ziemba, author of the book *When Football Was Football: The Chicago Cardinals and the Birth of the NFL.*

The Etceteras

An expert on nonbaseball events at Wrigley is George Castle, who wrote fascinating articles on the subject in Cubs souvenir programs in the 1980s. The description of the 1915 hippodrome at Weeghman Park is from *Sporting Life*, a weekly baseball newspaper that is now defunct.

The Celebrities

The Ronald Reagan radio story comes from *So You Think You're a Die-Hard Cubs Fan* by Bob Logan. The account of Reagan at Wrigley Field is based on articles by Bill McAllister and Tom Shales in the *Washington Post*. Articles in the *Chicago Sun-Times* and *Detroit News* aptly describe the Hillary Clinton appearance. For Bill Murray's hijinks, Joel Bierig in the *Sun-Times* and Mike Downey in the *Los Angeles Times* are the best sources.

PART IV: HOW IT WORKS

The Crew

The Paul Friedman quote is from a Jeff Favre article in the *Chicago Tribune*. Many of the Pat Pieper details come from Ed Hartig's December 1999 article in *Vine Line* and John Husar's obituary of Pieper in the *Chicago Tribune*.

The Concessions

An article by Bob Ibach in a 1987 Cubs souvenir program details the distance vendors used to walk and the calls they used to use. The adjustment for inflation for concession prices and salaries is based on a table done by Professor Robert Sahr of Oregon State University's political science department. Vendor John Jackanicz, while not quoted directly in this book, was an excellent source on how concessions work.

The Tickets

The "second row only" story is from a Chris McNamara article in the *Chicago Reader.*

Hidden Wrigley

Some of the Bobby Dorr information is from an Ed Burns article in *The Sporting News.*

PART V: LEGACY

Special Moments

Doug Myers's *Essential Cubs* is a wonderful source of details on Wrigley's special moments as well as of funny quotes and great statistics. A host of newspapers contributed to the tales related here, including the *Chicago Tribune* (Fred Mitchell, Paul Sullivan, Terry Armour, Bernie Lincicome, and George Langford), *Chicago Sun-Times* (Jerome Holtzman), *San Francisco Chronicle* (C. W. Nevius), and *Los Angeles Times* (Mike Downey). The book *Chicago Days* includes a deftly written essay by Alan Solomon on the "Called Shot." Other sources are *Tales from the Cubs Dugout* by Pete Cava; *The Golden Era Cubs* and *The New Era Cubs* by Eddie Gold and Art Ahrens; and *The Chicago Cubs: Memories and Memorabilia of the Wrigley Wonders,* text by Bruce Chadwick, photography by David M. Spindel. *Take Me Out to the Cubs Game* by John C. Skipper has an excellent account of the "two balls in play" incident. In various books, there is disagreement over the exact itinerary of the baseballs in the "two balls in play" incident. Alvin Dark said Delmore gave ball number two to the catcher, Taylor, while Myers reports that Delmore gave the ball to the pitcher, Anderson. Second-base umpire Bill Jackowski said the ball was given to Taylor, who gave it to Anderson. We're going with the ump on this one. The Pete Rose quote is from Curt Smith's *Storied Stadiums*. The Jim Riggleman quote is from Carrie Muskat's *Banks to Sandberg to Grace*. And a footnote on Hartnett's homer: *gloaming* is a Middle English word meaning "twilight."

Tributes

The details on the Harry Caray statue, including the quotes of Dutchie and Chip Caray and Steve Stone, are from Toni Ginnetti's article in the *Chicago Sun-Times*.

The Future

The Pat Gillick quote is taken from George Castle's *The Million-to-One Team*. The George Will quote about Williamsburg comes from the *Chicago Sun-Times*'s fine coverage of Wrigley's big night on August 8, 1988. The Jack Brickhouse quote is from Curt Smith's *Storied Stadiums*.

225

PHOTO CREDITS

In the early 1920s, the Chicago Cubs' official photographer was Francis Burke, whose work is now part of the David Phillips Collection. Before the 1929 season, members of the Cubs wanted their pictures taken, so they sought out Burke but by mistake called another photographer named Burke—George Burke. The new Burke caught on so well that the Cubs never went back to that other Burke named Francis, who doubtless was mystified that he never got more work from the Cubs. George Burke's assistant was George Brace, and the two of them were official photographers for the Cubs until 1948, when George Burke retired. Brace gave up his role as official photographer but kept taking baseball photos until the mid-'90s. In the '50s, Barney Sterling succeeded Burke and Brace as the official photographer, but much of Sterling's work was in motion pictures, not stills. Freelancers such as Fran Byrne added to the Cubs' photo archive. In 1981, a newcomer named Stephen Green prowled the park, shooting only black-and-white photos under an Illinois Arts Council grant. (The photo at left is Green's only black-and-white photo in this book.) After a season at the park, Green became the Cubs' official photographer, switched to color, and in 2002 marked his 20th anniversary in that role. This book is a celebration of his two-decade labor of love.

"It's our home. It's where we belong. It's where we were all raised. Yeah, the floor creaks and there are noises in the attic, but this is where we belong."

—John McDonough, Cubs vice president for marketing and broadcasting

INDEX